Living the Legacy

A collection of feature stories, news articles, and commentaries examining race and education today, including results from two national polls.

ISBN 0-9674795-2-5

To order copies of this book,
Telephone: (800) 346-1834
Fax: (301) 280-3250
Or write: EDUCATION WEEK PRESS
6935 Arlington Road, Suite 100
Bethesda, MD 20814

Visit us on the Web at edweek.org.

Also from EDUCATION WEEK PRESS:

Building Bridges With the Press: A Guide for Educators

*Miles To Go ... Reflections on Mid-Course Corrections
For Standards-Based Reform*

Lessons of a Century: A Nation's Schools Come of Age

Cover photograph by Allison Shelley
Kishona Leonard, a 2nd grader at St. Paul Primary School
in Summerton, S.C., listens to her teacher read a story.

CONTENTS

As part of our coverage of the 50th anniversary of the *Brown* v. *Board of Education of Topeka* decision, *Education Week* worked with Harris Interactive of Rochester, N.Y., to survey American adults' views on race and education. The responses to each question asked on the national survey are available online, including response rates specific to demographic, racial, and ethnic subgroups participating in the survey.

See www.edweek.org/sreports/brownpoll.pdf.

Race still matters in American education. Disparities in achievement remain, as does racial isolation in places such as Summerton, S.C.

Where It All Began

Summerton, S.C., was one of the birthplaces of the movement to desegregate public schools.

Black families fed up with the indignities of substandard schools and the lack of transportation for their children to attend them banded together in the rural community. With the help of lawyers from the National Association for the Advancement of Colored People—including Thurgood Marshall—they filed a lawsuit challenging the status quo.

That suit, *Briggs* v. *Elliott*, was one of four that were consolidated by the U.S. Supreme Court into the *Brown* v. *Board of Education of Topeka* case.

Any assessment of how far the nation has come since the 1954 decision striking down segregated schools must take Summerton into account. But by any measure, the movement that began here so promisingly ended up bringing little change to Summerton's schools.

Today, they still are overwhelmingly black and poor.

First graders at St. Paul Primary School, a public school in Summerton, S.C., read in the library.

Allison Shelley

Joseph C. Elliott, a grandson of the school board chairman challenged in *Briggs* v. *Elliott* and a former headmaster of the town's private academy, stands on the porch of the house his family has occupied for seven generations.

Stuck in Time

The movement to desegregate precollegiate education got its start in Summerton, S.C. But then it passed right on by.

The Rev. Melvin J. Capers walks through a graveyard at Liberty Hill AME Church, where some of the plaintiffs in the lawsuit are buried.

LOCAL LEADERS

The Rev. Joseph A. De Laine, third from left, meets with religious leaders at his church in Lake City, S.C. At great cost to himself and his family, De Laine worked closely with top state and national leaders of the NAACP to secure a better education for black children in Clarendon County.

BY ALAN RICHARD

Photographs by Allison Shelley

Summerton, S.C.

Fifty-five years ago, the Rev. Joseph A. De Laine and some of his followers in this South Carolina town decided they'd had enough. Enough walking or catching their children a ride several miles for school, since no bus was provided for black children. Enough of a high school principal they believed was corrupt. Enough of a bad education at the hands of white leaders who happened to be their neighbors and bosses.

They met in the churches of Summerton and the flat farmland around Clarendon County, and their courage helped propel the legal movement for equality in American precollegiate education.

With the filing in 1950 of *Briggs* v. *Elliott*, a lawsuit that was the first of four consolidated into *Brown* v. *Board of Education of Topeka,* families from this little town would make their mark on history. The battle they started here with petitions in the late 1940s helped desegregate public schools and paved the way for the Civil Rights Act of 1964.

What it did not do was change the way Summerton educates its young people.

Here in this birthplace of the school desegregation movement, integration has failed. Fifty years after the U.S. Supreme Court's decision in the *Brown* case—and more than three decades after many South Carolina public schools integrated—black and white students in

Summerton mostly do not mix.

Only 2 percent of the students in Summerton'spublic schools are white—a percentage has not changed much in 30 years. They number about two dozen of the more than 1,100 students in the town's public schools, in a county where about 60 percent of the residents are black.

The vast majority of white students here attend Clarendon Hall, a small, private academy that opened in the mid-1960s for white families ready to flee the public schools as implementation of the *Brown* decision finally arrived.

The public and private schools operate in a town with two stoplights and only 900 people, where fears and resentments stirred by the desegregation case still linger. Some residents here lament that the economy and local society have changed little since De Laine and his flock dared to challenge Summerton's separate, unequal way of life.

HOWARD STERLING'S 2ND GRADERS at the public St. Paul Primary School gasped when a visitor told them that it was once against the law for black and white students to attend school together.

A few mouths dropped open as they listened to stories about De Laine, who once led parent meetings at a church within walking distance of their school outside Summerton. The De Laine family's home burned while firemen watched, and the minister and teacher fled South Carolina in 1955 after he returned gunfire aimed at his house. Later a minister in New York state, he would be a wanted man in his home

state for decades.

A boy in Sterling's class raised his hand to ask: "That really happened?"

Each one of the 20 or so children in the teacher's summer school class was African-American. "An integrated system would be stronger," says Patricia R. Middleton, the African-American principal at St. Paul Primary.

Many classes at St. Paul appear to be well-taught and the teachers motivated. But the

district, officially known as Clarendon County School District One, has problems. The Summerton public schools have posted low test scores for years, and administrative scandals have plagued the district.

The low-slung brick building that houses St. Paul Primary is too small, so portable classrooms fill the back lot. The restrooms, although clean and well-supplied, haven't been renovated in many years. Music and art teachers were let go last school year after state budget cuts.

Thomas Briggs, a 5th grader, left, and William Ziegler, a 6th grader, prepare to go onstage during Clarendon Hall's annual Christmas play.

The town's elementary school cut art and music, and the high school posted the state's lowest average SAT scores.

Nearly half the students who enroll in 9th grade at Scott's Branch High School, the district's only high school, don't graduate on time. Last year, the average combined SAT score at Scott's Branch dipped to 761 out of a possible 1600—the lowest average of any high school in South Carolina.

Still, there are signs the public schools are doing better. St. Paul Primary in November learned of vastly improved test scores, becoming the first school in the community to earn a "good" rating on state report cards.

THE PICTURE ISN'T NEARLY AS BLEAK for Clarendon District Two, a 3,500-student district that encompasses the county seat of Manning.

Manning is a vibrant little town of about 4,000 residents, some seven miles from Summerton, with a traditional square around the courthouse and a series of new businesses stretching toward Interstate 95. There's a new commercial strip that includes a car dealership and fast-food places.

The public schools in Manning are larger and in better shape than Summerton's. Manning High School, the centerpiece, has a statue of its Monarch lion mascot standing on a giant lawn in front of the building. The football stadium

Jaquan Johnson, a kindergarten student at St. Paul Primary School in Summerton, starts his day with a breakfast provided by the school.

behind the school is large and impressive enough for some universities.

Today, the Manning district's enrollment is about 70 percent black. The diversity in the schools closely mirrors the racial makeup of the local population. Test scores in the Manning schools are about average compared with those in the rest of the state.

Local leaders attribute the integration of the schools to several influential white families, including that of state Sen. John Land and his wife, Marie, who kept their children enrolled

and urged others to do the same.

Marie Land campaigned for a bond vote that helped renovate schools and paid for a new jewel: the Manning Early Childhood Center. The sprawling campus boasts skylights, and colorful columns inside that look like huge stacks of children's blocks.

Summerton school leaders were so impressed with the new school in Manning that Clarendon District One decided to build an early-childhood center of its own. But money ran short, and the structure stands half-finished behind the district office.

Students here in Summerton know that the enrollment in Manning and other towns is more integrated than their district's, and they sometimes question the quality of the education they receive.

Jonathan Henry, a junior at Scott's Branch High whose great-great-grandfather, Gilbert H. Henry, was a plaintiff in *Briggs* v. *Elliott*, has heard about the movement to desegregate schools from his relatives. He seems bewildered, though, when asked about his interactions with white students. He doesn't really know any.

A girl he knows in Manning has spoken of her white classmates, he offers. "She [has been] telling me there's not any difference

11

Collective Action

Briggs v. ***Elliott***, the lawsuit filed in Clarendon County, S.C., was one of four cases that became known collectively as ***Brown*** v. ***Board of Education of Topeka***.

The U.S. Supreme Court consolidated the cases in 1952, when it agreed to hear appeals in each of them and in a fifth case against segregation in the District of Columbia schools. Lawyers for the National Association for the Advancement of Colored People, under future Supreme Court Justice Thurgood Marshall, led the legal fight.

The *Brown* lawsuit challenged the Topeka, Kan., board of education's decision to establish segregated elementary schools under a state law that permitted, but did not require, cities of 15,000 residents or more to maintain separate school facilities for black and white children. The other public schools in the community weren't segregated, notes the author Richard Kluger in the 1977 book *Simple Justice*, a definitive account of the case.

A three-judge federal panel in the Kansas case found that segregation had a detrimental affect on black children. But it denied relief to the plaintiffs—including Oliver Brown, suing on behalf of his daughter Linda—because it found that schools for blacks and whites were substantially equal in their buildings, transportation, curricula, and teachers' educational levels. The ruling was then appealed to the Supreme Court.

The Virginia case, ***Davis*** v. ***County School Board of Prince Edward County***, involved a challenge by black high school students to the state's required segregation in public schools.

As was true in the South Carolina complaint, a federal court found that the physical facilities for black students were inferior and ordered them to be made equal to those for white children. But the court denied black students access to whites-only schools while the problems were addressed. Both federal courts also turned back the plaintiffs' challenges to the underlying constitutionality of segregated schools.

The fourth case was ***Gebhart*** v. ***Belton***, brought by black children in New Castle County, Del. A state court ordered that black students be admitted to the all-white schools, and the state supreme court affirmed the ruling. State officials appealed to the U.S. Supreme Court.

The District of Columbia case, ***Bolling*** v. ***Sharpe***, challenged segregation under the due-process clause of the Fifth Amendment to the U.S. Constitution, rather than under the equal-protection clause of the 14th Amendment as the other cases had done. (That approach stemmed from Washington's status as a federal city, not a state.)

But as the Supreme Court declared in its May 17, 1954, opinion in the case: "Discrimination may be so unjustifiable as to be violative of due process." —ANN BRADLEY

in personality and things they like to do," Henry says.

Natasha Lemon, an 11th grader at Scott's Branch who plays every sport and is a drummer in the school band, wishes the local schools and community offered more. She learned at a summer camp about dance, music, and French. "I'm so in love with it," she says of the language. But her school offers only Spanish, and the other subjects are limited because the same teacher juggles drama, English, and art, she says.

Lemon hears of schools elsewhere that have laptop computers, swimming pools, and paved running tracks. As for integration, she says, Scott's Branch has only a handful of students who aren't black. "We're so blocked off from each other," she says.

Superintendent Clarence Willie, now in his second year at Clarendon One, has named three new principals, smoothed out recent budget problems, and set higher academic goals. Integration would help the schools, he says, but isn't what he was hired to do.

"My job is to run the best school system, according to the laws and policies, the best that I can," says Willie, an African-American administrator who was hired after a career in North Carolina public schools. He's now pushing for a town vote on a tax increase that would help finish the early-childhood center and move St. Paul Primary's students into the new school.

The superintendent adds that a new economic catalyst would help Summerton change and grow. He pins his hopes on Lake Marion, a couple of miles away. The lake's swampy fringes make for great fishing, which has stirred development across the lake.

Joseph A. De Laine Jr., a son of the minister who helped lead the fight for educational equality in Clarendon County, sits outside the Briggs-De Laine-Pearson Foundation. Started by families with ties to *Briggs* v. *Elliott*, the foundation plans to open a display of historical exhibits related to the case.

Summerton is beginning to come to grips with history, although black and white residents still keep their distance.

State Rep. Alex Harvin III, whose family has played a leading role in white Summerton for generations, says he has tried during some 30 years in the South Carolina legislature to work for the town's economic development. He has had little luck, while suburban and coastal areas of the state boom.

CLARENDON HALL OPENED IN 1965 at the Summerton First Baptist Church as a private school for students working toward college and professional careers. Everyone in Summerton knows, though, that the school was started for one reason—in anticipation of school integration, which finally came in 1970.

Today, Clarendon Hall enrolls about 275 students in preschool through 12th grade. The first two black students ever to attend the school enrolled in the 2001-02 school year, officials say. This year, the school has five African-American students.

The traditional lack of racial diversity was immediately apparent to Headmaster Michael "Doc" Connors and his wife, Pat, a preschool teacher. The couple retired here in 1999 after long teaching careers in Tully, N.Y. Michael Connors taught science and math at Clarendon Hall and coached football and track before becoming headmaster two years ago.

When he arrived, he thought it natural that Clarendon Hall students would play Scott's Branch High in sports. The schools are only a couple of miles apart. He helped organize a preseason basketball scrimmage, and at first, didn't realize the importance of what he was doing.

" 'Black kids are playing white kids on the same basketball court for the first time in history,' " Connors recalls someone telling him. "I was sort of taken aback by the whole thing."

Clarendon Hall is a building of well-kept, modest classroom wings connected by outdoor breezeways. Connors is leading a $1 million building campaign to renovate the campus, including the addition of a white-columned entrance and office area. Most of the teachers are experienced and certified, but earn only about $17,000 a year, with no benefits.

Tuition runs about $2,600. No scholarships are available, but members of the school's board and other benefactors donate generously, Connors says, when families need help with the costs. Mostly, families choose Clarendon Hall for the smaller classes, the evangelical Christian emphasis, and the strict discipline policies, he says.

More minority students are welcome at Clarendon Hall, he adds, but he's not sure how many will end up enrolling. "I'm pleased; I think everybody is pleased," he says of the new arrivals.

JOSEPH C. ELLIOTT SERVED AS THE HEADMASTER of Clarendon Hall from 1999 until he hired the current headmaster in 2002.

A grandson of R.M. Elliott—the school board chairman who was the lead defendant in *Briggs* v. *Elliott*—he lives down a dirt lane outside Summerton, lined with a tunnel of oaks draped with Spanish moss. The old Cantey house where he dwells has been in his mother's family for seven generations.

Harry Briggs, who sued Elliott's paternal grandfather in the case, grew up on the property. Elliott grew up knowing Briggs' parents as "Uncle Ned" and "Aunt Laura." Elliott's father later bulldozed their little tin-roofed house, which could be seen from the front porch of the larger home. "Harry Briggs' mother was the maid in this house for 40 or 50 years," Elliott says.

Although he is clearly part of the old guard in Summerton, Elliott says his experiences as a teacher and administrator in public schools elsewhere have left him with moderate views on race.

A history buff who has taught college classes, Elliott is concerned that some white leaders in Summerton are remembered only as racists. There was more to them than that, he says. "The hero in all this was certainly not my grandfather," he acknowledges, adding, "He did what was expected of him."

He remembers his grandfather as a man of great physical strength who would kindly give his grandchildren pocket change. Not formally educated, R.M. Elliott owned a lumber company in town and dabbled in cotton gins and farming.

Joseph Elliott's mother's side of the family is believed to have given the Briggs family food after their supplies and employment were cut off in the bitter aftermath of the case. "I think it took some courage to do so," Elliott says.

However, he's also concerned that white people in Summerton don't respect or understand the courage it took for the black plaintiffs to challenge segregation. When he talks about that view, "old friends look away," Elliott says.

The continuing separation of the races here, he believes, is partly due to hard feelings engendered by the lawsuit.

"Segregation in Summerton does hang on the case," he says, but also is complicated by the relatively poor quality of the public schools, racial bias, and cultural and class differences.

For black families, he says, whites' silence about the case "translates to them as a belief among whites that they believe in segregation still."

SUMMERTON IS GRADUALLY BEGINNING to recognize itself as the birthplace of the legal action that culminated in the historic *Brown* decision in May 1954. Plenty of people here want the schools to do better and for the local economy to pick up steam. The lack of change, many here agree, isn't benefiting anyone.

Willie, the Summerton superintendent, and Connors of Clarendon Hall have joined economic-development committees trying to revive the downtown. They're also discussing more joint school activities.

The Briggs-De Laine-Pearson Foundation, created in part by three children of the Rev.

Longtime Summerton residents Mary Truesdale, left, Joyce Hill, and Carol Myers enjoy breakfast at the Summerton Diner. Most of the restaurant's patrons are white.

Joseph A. De Laine, holds banquets to celebrate *Briggs* v. *Elliott* and is raising money for a building that will house historical exhibits related to the landmark case.

Local signs of progress include the Fishers of Men, an interracial Christian men's group that meets monthly in Summerton churches for cookouts, prayers, and fellowship. On a Saturday morning last summer, a dozen or more men, black and white, joined hands in prayer at each school in Summerton.

"We ask for togetherness, Lord, because togetherness is what we need," prayed Aaron Jones, a member of Liberty Hill African Methodist Episcopal Church, where De Laine and others once met to organize against the local school leaders.

But even in the prayer group, there were signs of separation. At Clarendon Hall, a white man thanked God for the "men and women who had the vision" to start the school, and "for the virtues and the morals of these kids here."

At Scott's Branch High, there were prayers among some of the white men to "change the culture" of the school, for students to save their "virtues" until marriage, and for the students to respect their elders.

Asked if the men's group means that the barriers that have separated white and black here for so long may be finally lifting, organizer Val Elliott, a cousin of Joseph C. Elliott, says he isn't so sure. "It's going to take some more time," he says.

Fifty years, and Summerton needs just a little more time. ∎

Charlotte, N.C., was considered the "city that made desegregation work." But today, more schools are becoming racially imbalanced.

After the Buses Stop Rolling

Once the U.S. Supreme Court declared separate schooling for black and white students unconstitutional in its May 17, 1954, ruling in *Brown* v. *Board of Education of Topeka*, it was up to school districts to figure out how to integrate classrooms.

In Charlotte-Mecklenburg, N.C., the answer was busing. A 1971 Supreme Court decision upheld that strategy and cleared the way for districts nationwide to use mandatory busing to desegregate schools.

As a result, the district once boasted some of the nation's most integrated classrooms.

But today, it is no longer permitted to use race in deciding where students attend classes—a reflection of changes in the legal and social tenor of the times that have seen desegregation efforts wane nationwide.

As a result, some Charlotte schools are much less racially diverse than they were in the heyday of integration. But the district is also making gains in raising black students' test scores.

The Charlotte-Mecklenburg, N.C., district became a national symbol for busing when the U.S. Supreme Court upheld that strategy for integration.

Allison Shelley

Jessica Sansevero, left, and Gina Alexander flip through a yearbook during a fair sponsored by the Charlotte-Mecklenburg district in January 2004 to help families select schools.

Color Bind

Three decades ago, a legal decision involving Charlotte, N.C., paved the way for mandatory busing nationwide. Now, integration depends on where you live.

The rapid growth of the suburbs in Mecklenburg County is causing overcrowding and calls from parents for more school construction.

INTEGRATION BEGINS

Dorothy Counts, 15, one of the first black students to attend Harding High School in Charlotte, N.C., is taunted by white students as she is escorted home from school on Sept. 5, 1957. Eight years later, black families sued the district, seeking desegregated schools.

BY KARLA SCOON REID

Photographs by Allison Shelley

Charlotte, N.C.

Something is different about the children gazing out the windows of the yellow school buses lumbering up Selwyn Elementary School's driveway: Most of the black faces are gone.

White children have taken the places of many of the African-American students who were bused to Selwyn, once an integrated school in the heart of one of this city's oldest and wealthiest white neighborhoods.

The Charlotte-Mecklenburg school district, free from a federal desegregation order, adopted a colorblind plan for student assignment in 2002 that is producing more racially isolated schools, like Selwyn, and more schools enrolling high concentrations of poor children.

From the mid-1970s through the 1980s, the North Carolina school system made up of Charlotte and surrounding Mecklenburg County earned national acclaim as the "city that made desegregation work." The key was a landmark 1971 ruling by the U.S. Supreme Court, in *Swann v. Charlotte-Mecklenburg Board of Education*, that cleared the way for Charlotte—and districts nationwide—to use mandatory busing and race-based student assignment as tools to achieve integration. Now, many observers wonder whether Charlotte-Mecklenburg's school buses are headed in the right direction.

The Charlotte-Mecklenburg district is gaining ground academically, but sliding on measures of integration.

"Charlotte is stumbling and it's falling," laments Roslyn Arlin Mickelson, a professor of sociology at the University of North Carolina at Charlotte. "In a couple of years, in terms of racial composition of the schools, the district is going to be back where it was prior to *Swann*."

The 2-year-old plan gives parents a choice of schools and provides all families with spots in the "neighborhood schools" closest to their homes. Since parents overwhelmingly choose their local schools, the district's 148 schools are becoming more racially and socioeconomically imbalanced. Suburban classrooms are overcrowded, and seats are left empty in inner-city schools.

This inevitable demographic shift, some observers say, shouldn't rattle the resolve of the "New Charlotte," a Southern city that rejected its segregated education practices long ago to emerge as a beacon for integration.

But others warn that the enrollment changes are derailing the racial progress that led to the region's economic boom and laid the foundation for its students' academic successes. This school year, 43 percent of the district's 116,800 students are African-American; 42 percent are white; 9 percent are Hispanic; and 7 percent are Asian-American, American Indian, or multiracial.

Superintendent James L. Pughsley acknowledges that the system faces a crossroads: "Are we going to be one of those large, urban districts that allowed themselves to slip behind? We don't have to be. We have a chance to define our destiny."

Teresa Hermanson plays with her sons Kevin, 6, left, and Marcus, 3, at their suburban home. She faults the district for repeated changes in where students are assigned to attend school.

A white parent, William Capacchione, sued the school system in 1997, alleging that its race-based admissions policy for magnet schools was unconstitutional. That lawsuit eventually led to the reactivation of the *Swann* case. In 2001, the U.S. Court of Appeals for the 4th Circuit, in Richmond, Va., affirmed a lower-court ruling that Charlotte's schools were free of the vestiges of segregation. The U.S. Supreme Court declined to review the case the following year.

What followed, some observers caution, could undo the gains Charlotte made during the years of desegregation.

"The Charlotte-Mecklenburg system may be

allowing individual choice by parents to take such a predominant role, without doing the social math and looking at the communitywide impact of those decisions," says Jack Boger, the deputy director of the University of North Carolina's center for civil rights in Chapel Hill. "The system will become terribly segregated—with no single person having done a wicked thing."

RACIAL RATIOS ASIDE, THE DISTRICT IS GAINING GROUND in closing the differences in achievement between students of different races. That, many argue, is the critical—yet

A student walks past an industrial area next to Charlotte's Marie G. Davis Middle School, which was once an integrated magnet school. Now serving the neighborhood, its enrollment is 95 percent black and 92 percent poor.

Timeline

July 1960 The school districts of Charlotte and Mecklenburg County merge.

January 1965 Ten black families, including lead plaintiffs Vera and Darius Swann, sue the Charlotte-Mecklenburg district to obligate it to desegregate its schools. The case is known as *Swann* v. *Charlotte-Mecklenburg Board of Education*.

April 1969 U.S. District Judge James B. McMillan orders the district to draw up a plan for the "effective desegregation" of the pupil population, which could include mandatory busing. The following fall, the district's efforts to integrate schools by busing children is marked by turmoil and violence.

April 1971 The U.S. Supreme Court upholds Judge McMillan's decision in the *Swann* case. The ruling allows school systems nationwide to use mandatory busing and other race-based efforts to desegregate public schools.

October 1984 Campaigning for a second term, President Ronald Reagan says in a speech in Charlotte: "[Busing] takes innocent children out of the neighborhood school and makes them pawns in a social experiment that nobody wants."

March 1992 The school board approves Superintendent John Murphy's plan to eliminate portions of the district's mandatory-busing program and establish magnet schools.

September 1997 White parent William Capacchione sues the district, claiming its race-based admission policy is unconstitutional, after his daughter is denied entry to a magnet school because of her race.

March 1998 U.S. District Judge Robert D. Potter reactivates the *Swann* case. Later that year, six white parents join the challenge to the student-assignment policies; two black families join the *Swann* plaintiffs to try to maintain desegregation efforts.

September 1999 Judge Potter declares the system free of all vestiges of segregation, and orders the district to end its race-based student-assignment plans. "Essentially, [the district] is 'standing in the schoolhouse door' and turning students away from its magnet programs based on race," he writes.

September 2001 A full panel of the U.S. Court of Appeals for the 4th Circuit, in Richmond, Va., affirms the lower-court ruling that the district has achieved unitary status.

April 2002 The Supreme Court declines without comment to review the case. The race-neutral plan begins in August.

unmet—goal of the Supreme Court's decision in *Brown* v. *Board of Education of Topeka*, which struck down separate systems of schooling for black and white students. May 17 will mark the 50th anniversary of that historic 1954 ruling.

"We've learned that desegregation is not the pathway to closing the achievement gap," says David J. Armor, a professor of public policy at George Mason University in Fairfax, Va. "Desegregation doesn't take the place of better teachers and smaller classes, or whatever one does to improve the achievement of minority children and poor children."

Eric J. Smith, who served as the superintendent here from 1996 to 2002, says that after more than 20 years of busing, disparities among Charlotte-Mecklenburg schools persisted, from the condition of facilities to the quality of teachers. Smith, now the superintendent of the Anne Arundel County, Md., schools, says most black students—whether they attended desegregated schools or not—were not making the grade.

Smith credits the *Brown* decision for moving public education in the nation forward, but says educators today face a different challenge. "If we in America can't get schools with high concentrations of poverty to succeed," he asks, "then what does that say about the major cities populated primarily with children from low-income families?"

The former Charlotte superintendent established an equity program that each year pumps millions of dollars into high-poverty schools in an attempt to boost test scores. Last year, the district allocated roughly $40 million to equity efforts, including teacher-pay incentives and smaller class sizes.

The investments appear to be paying off. On national and state tests, results show the district is making headway in reducing the gap that finds African-American and Hispanic students lagging behind their white and Asian-American peers.

Pughsley, the district's current chief, points out: "The reason 'separate and equal' never worked was because it was never equal. We've moved from equal opportunity to equal results."

THE ADDITIONAL MONEY SPENT to produce those "equal results" in the classroom could be in jeopardy, however.

Suburban parents are growing impatient with crowded classrooms and are lobbying hard for new schools. The Mecklenburg County Commission, which provides roughly a third of the district's $887 million annual budget, is run by a Republican majority that has supported tax cuts and hasn't increased school funding for the past two years. Some residents also believe the newly elected school board will siphon off dollars directed to low-performing schools to meet parents' demands.

"It's like having the worst of both worlds," declares Stephen Samuel Smith, a professor of political science at Winthrop University in Rock Hill, S.C. "The system will be resegregated, and we're not going to have the resources that have been promised."

Nancy D. Beasley, the principal of Selwyn Elementary, worries about the black students who didn't return to her classrooms after the race-based assignment plan was dropped two years ago.

Since 2001, Selwyn's black enrollment has decreased by more than half, from 34 percent to 16 percent of its 526 students this year. The percentage of students eligible for free or reduced-price lunches, an indicator of family income, fell from 31 percent to 16 percent.

Most of the pupils who left Selwyn now attend schools with large numbers of poor children. Their class sizes may be smaller, but Beasley says she regrets that the students won't receive the benefits, such as an active PTA and business partners, that are typical of a school with a more integrated population.

Using enrollment figures for 2003-04, Mickelson of UNC-Charlotte found that 33 percent of the district's schools were racially balanced, compared with 52 percent in 2001, the final year of race-based assignments. The number of schools where the percentage of students receiving free or reduced-price lunches exceeded 50 percent climbed from 53 in 2001 to 76 in 2003, according to the district. About 44 percent of the district's students qualify for lunch subsidies.

The system tried to maintain socioeconomic and racial diversity through parental choice, says Eric J. Becoats, an assistant superintendent for planning and development. But most suburban parents chose their neighborhood schools. And with 4,000 new students joining the rolls this past fall, most schools were overcrowded, leaving few vacant seats for parents seeking different schools for their children.

In fact, just before 5,000 people entered the district's annual school information fair in January, officials dropped the word "choice" from the application guide for the 2004-05 school year.

Arthur Griffin Jr., the former chairman of the school board, visits West Charlotte High School. Griffin is concerned that board members no longer value diversity.

An expanding population and tight budgets are likely to force hard decisions on how to make schooling equal for all.

"Unless we get rid of the home-school guarantee," Becoats cautions, referring to neighborhood schools, "we're not going to deal with the concentration of poor and minority kids."

WITHDRAWAL OF THE PLEDGE to back neighborhood schools is extremely unlikely.

A vocal and well-organized crop of suburban parents insists that school feeder patterns remain stable. Parent activists backed two newly elected school board members who are staunch supporters of the neighborhood-school guarantee, creating a majority on the nine-member board.

Teresa Hermanson, who moved to Charlotte's southern suburbs five years ago, believes the system's preoccupation with race-based assignment led to fractured communities. Over nine years, she says, the elementary school attendance zone in her neighborhood has changed five times.

Hermanson, a white stay-at-home mother with traces of a Long Island, N.Y., accent, organized Parents for Education in Charlotte-Mecklenburg Schools last year. The group advocates high-quality schools and a consistent pupil-assignment plan that addresses the growing student population—issues that she says transcend race.

Largely missing from the neighborhood-schools debate are the voices of African-Americans—once the conscience of the struggle for integrated schools in Charlotte-Mecklenburg. While desegregation advocates are dispirited by the legal defeat here, some black parents say they find themselves torn between pushing for better-quality schools and seeking ways to foster integration.

"You can't sacrifice a child's academic opportunity for diversity," says Jay Ferguson, an African-American parent of three whose father, James E. Ferguson II, represented the black plaintiffs in the *Swann* case. A 1988 graduate of an integrated Charlotte high school, Ferguson says parents shouldn't be forced to make that agonizing choice.

A newly formed group of advocates for integration and school equality held a protest here late last month, outside an exhibit commemorating the *Brown* decision at the Levine Museum of the New South. Members of the group believe the promise of equal schools for all remains unfulfilled. One founder, Richard A. McElrath, a retired Charlotte teacher, says if the city's schools continue to become racially isolated, then "the money will follow the white children. That's just a fact of life."

ARTHUR GRIFFIN JR., THE FORMER CHAIRMAN of the Charlotte-Mecklenburg school board, can't hide his dismay as he walks the hallways of West Charlotte High School, once the crown jewel in the city's desegregation efforts.

Roughly an hour after three new members were sworn in on Dec. 9, the board reversed student-assignment decisions. They contended that the changes were minor and, in some cases, would help preserve the neighborhood-school philosophy. But other board members argued the shifts would exacerbate racial and economic isolation in some schools.

For Griffin, whose soft-spoken manner belies his strong beliefs, the board's actions on the night he made his farewell remarks represented his worst fears. "It sends a message to the community that diversity no longer matters," says Griffin, a 17-year board veteran who vowed not to lead the board that "resegregates" Charlotte's schools and did not seek re-election last year.

Griffin has only to glance around West Charlotte High to see how much the district has changed since the heyday of integration in the early 1980s. This year, roughly 90 percent of the 1,500 students here are black; about 3 percent are white.

White politicians and business leaders once sent their children to West Charlotte High with children from the affluent and middle-income black families who lived nearby, says Amy Stuart Wells, a professor of sociology and education at Teachers College, Columbia University.

"West Charlotte is the symbol of the rise and fall of desegregation in Charlotte-Mecklenburg," says Wells, who is completing a study of the graduates of the class of 1980 in integrated high schools across the nation, including West Charlotte.

Griffin charges that concessions that he and other board members made on student assignment were followed by broken promises, as the district yielded to the mounting pressures of a growing enrollment and assertive parents—many of them newcomers to Charlotte—who were opposed to busing.

"People always talk about their commitment to diversity," says Griffin, who is the vice president for national urban markets at the McGraw-Hill Education Co. "But the same people would wink and look the other way when tough decisions were made about pupil assignment."

Economic and population growth in the district's far north and south regions strained efforts to desegregate schools. From 1990 to 2000, the county added about 148,000 new residents, making it the 25th-fastest-growing county in the United States. About 800,000 people now live in Mecklenburg County.

Ironically, Smith of Winthrop University argues that without school desegregation, Charlotte would not have developed into the nation's second-largest banking center. Still, he says, business leaders failed to help preserve the district's integration efforts as highways and residential communities were developed away from its urban core.

"Development trumped desegregation every time," argues Smith, the author of *Boom for Whom? Education, Desegregation, and Development in Charlotte*, which will be published in April.

Jay Ferguson and his daughter Johari, 3, admire a stained-glass window at Greenville Memorial AME Zion Church. His father represented the black families who sued the district to integrate its schools. Parents, Ferguson says, shouldn't be forced to choose between high-quality schools and diversity.

Kit Cramer, who is the group vice president for education at the Charlotte Chamber and the school board's new vice chairwoman, says the primary motivation of developers is understandably to make money. She adds, however, that the local business community has a long history of strong support for public schools.

Shifting to an assignment plan based on neighborhood schools wasn't a matter of caving to the demands of well-connected suburban parents, she insists, but an act of self-preservation.

"If you don't take into account the desires of individual parents, you lose them," Cramer warns. "You lose their vote on bond issues, you lose their tax dollars, and the tremendous support they generate."

Cramer says the community has no choice but to both build new schools and give high-poverty schools additional resources.

But board member Larry Gauvreau, who was one of the white parents who sued seeking an end to the desegregation plan, complains that the district is dedicating too much money to equity programs. "We're investing in the notion that social engineering is better than an educational course," he contends.

More than 30 years after school buses first began traveling Charlotte-Mecklenburg's roads in the name of integration, some people predict potholes along the new race-neutral course.

"The community has lost its will and its way," asserts James Ferguson, the lawyer who helped represent the black families in the desegregation case. "The community has to stand up for desegregation, or sit on its hands and watch the community become racially isolated." ∎

In Chicago, 36 percent of the students in public schools are Hispanic. School overcrowding, not integration, is the concern in Hispanic neighborhoods.

Chicago Hispanics Fight for Good Schools

In 1954, when the U.S. Supreme Court issued its historic ruling against school segregation in *Brown* v. *Board of Education of Topeka*, integration—to most Americans—was simply an issue of black and white.

Questions of race and ethnicity in the nation's education system were more complex even then, and today, Hispanic students outnumber African-American children in public schools. Court cases predicated on *Brown* have affirmed the right of Hispanic children to desegregated schooling, and of students whose first language is not English to receive extra help as they learn it.

But many parents and activists are still struggling for equal educational opportunity for Latino children. In Chicago's Little Village neighborhood, members of the nation's second-largest community of people of Mexican origin staged a dramatic, 19-day hunger strike in 2001 to secure the board of education's promise to build a new high school.

Gabrielle Diaz, a member of John Spry Elementary School's 32-student 9th grade class, earns "service hours" helping preschoolers select toys. In Chicago's Little Village, smaller schools have become a rallying cry.

Allison Shelley

Now, the building's skeletal outlines are taking shape. Residents say they hope the school's smaller, more personalized environment will offer students who would have had to leave the area to attend magnet schools a top-notch education—right in their own community.

Cynthia C. Nambo, a project director at the Little Village Community Development Corp., explains features of a new high school going up in a heavily Hispanic neighborhood of Chicago. Residents, including those pictured with Ms. Nambo, staged a hunger strike to urge that the school be built.

Close to Home

Chicago's public schools are now more than one-third Hispanic, reflecting the nation's demographic changes. Activists there are struggling for good schools.

Students at David G. Farragut Career Academy High School take down a flag.

Chicago

In 1954, when the U.S. Supreme Court handed down its decision in *Brown* v. *Board of Education of Topeka*, the South Lawndale neighborhood on Chicago's southwest side was home primarily to Polish and Czech immigrants.

In the decades since then, South Lawndale has undergone dramatic change. Eastern Europeans moved out, and people of Mexican descent settled in its two-story homes of brown brick. Known as Little Village, or *La Villita,* since the late 1960s, the neighborhood reflects demographic shifts that have changed the face of the nation in the 50 years since the historic court decision struck down racially segregated schooling.

Most adults in Little Village are first-generation Mexican immigrants, but many of their children were born in the United States. Chicago is home to the nation's second-largest community of people of Mexican origin, next only to Los Angeles.

Today, in fact, more than one-third of the 439,000 students attending the Chicago public schools are Hispanic. The enrollment of the nation's third-largest school district—in a Northern industrial city where Martin Luther King Jr. once marched to demand equal justice for black Americans—is now 51 percent black, 36 percent Hispanic, 9 percent white, 3 percent Asian-American, and less than 1 percent Native American.

UNREST OVER CIVIL RIGHTS

Members of the American Nazi Party demonstrate in August 1966 across from the Greater Mount Hope Baptist Church on Chicago's South Side. The Rev. Martin Luther King Jr. and other civil rights leaders met there to plan marches into white neighborhoods.

BY MARY ANN ZEHR

Photographs by Allison Shelley

Nationwide, Hispanic students have outnumbered African-American children in public schools since 1998. That trend has heightened the complexity of American education's demographic profile, after decades in which integration—in most people's eyes—was literally an issue of black and white. In Little Village, Latinos attend schools enrolling mostly minority students from poor families, reflecting a national pattern. Hispanic students are, "by most measures, the most segregated by both race and poverty," according to a recent report by Gary Orfield, a researcher at Harvard University.

King's last great community campaign was in Chicago, where the civil rights leader "hoped to change the racial inequities of the great urban complexes of the North," Orfield notes in his report. King led demonstrations against segregated schools and housing in the city, Orfield writes, but "there were no real triumphs and the basic patterns did not change."

Little Village's affordable housing—if not its schools—continues to attract new immigrants. Early waves of Mexican arrivals worked in factories making General Electric appliances and Brach's candy. Some immigrants still toil in factories, but many others board the No. 60 public bus for a 45-minute ride downtown to work in service jobs in Chicago's hotels and restaurants.

Signs of Mexican culture are everywhere in *La Villita*. A man belts out a Spanish love song while walking outside in subzero temperatures. *Piñatas* hang from the ceiling in a grocery store. Vendors at a "discount mall," set up like an indoor Mexican market, sell frilly pillows to carry the crown for a *quinceañera*, the 15th-birthday party customary for Mexican girls. Clocks are adorned with the image of Our Lady

Freshman Alondra Murillo salutes during a Junior ROTC class at John Spry Elementary, which added a 9th grade this year. Behind her is a mural depicting the emblem on the Mexican flag.

of Guadalupe, the Virgin Mary as she is said to have appeared as an indigenous Mexican woman in a 16th-century vision. A street vendor roasts *elotes*, or corn on the cob Mexican-style, over an open grill, while several kinds of steamed *tamales*, which melt in one's mouth, are available from Little Village's many restaurants.

BUT IN THIS NEIGHBORHOOD, WHEN RESIDENTS WANTED a new high school to relieve overcrowding and provide strong academics, they held a hunger strike to get one. Residents here believe Latinos have gotten short shrift when it comes to educational opportunities in Chicago.

Linda Sarate, a Texas-born Mexican-American who moved to Little Village at age 9 and is now a homemaker and mother of three, says she joined the 2001 hunger strike because she was angry that the district had promised a new high school for Little Village but never built it. What's more, the system had gone ahead and built two selective-enrollment high schools, which had also been promised in 1998, in wealthier neighborhoods.

"It was a slap in the face to the community, what they did," says Sarate, 46. "It was like they were saying, 'Your kids aren't worth it and my kids are.'"

But Arne Duncan, who became the chief executive officer of the Chicago school system only weeks after the hunger strike ended, says he would have made sure Little Village got a new high school even if there hadn't been a hunger strike.

Led by the Little Village Community Development Corp., residents struck for 19 days in the spring of 2001, until organizers called the protest off because of concerns for the strikers' health. Two months later, after Duncan succeeded Paul G. Vallas, the new district chief pledged to renew the 1998 promise.

"It was the right thing to do," Duncan says. "It's a community with a growing population. I saw tremendous need."

At long last, the new high school is going up. Expected to cost $61 million—more than any

In Chicago's heavily Hispanic Little Village, activists staged a hunger strike to plead for a new high school.

other public school in the city's history—it is scheduled to open in the fall of 2005 with a swimming pool, two gymnasiums, a health clinic, and a rooftop auditorium sheltered by a cone-shaped structure.

Duncan doesn't agree with the prevalent view in Little Village that the school system has discriminated against Latinos. Rather, he says, the district constantly faces the challenge of providing new schools in areas of the city where there is overcrowding, and "that is frequently in the Latino community."

The Little Village CDC has organized a committee to advise the district on the new high school to ensure that the facility will meet residents' needs. "Students in this neighborhood shouldn't have to go 10 miles to the North Side to go to a good high school," says Jaime de Leon, the coordinator of the effort by the Little Village CDC to help plan the new school. "We went to visit the North Side magnet schools and they had *all* these facilities. We said that we want what they've got."

Latino activists seem to view the city's long-standing patterns of segregation by race, ethnicity, and income level as difficult to change and outside their control.

"Kids are segregated in schools because housing is segregated," says Linda G. Coronado, a former Chicago school board member and a member of the Little Village CDC's advisory committee for the new high school. "The only people who can do anything

about that are elected officials."

Of the 1,400 students expected to attend the new school, as many as 75 percent likely will be Latinos; the remainder will be African-Americans from neighboring North Lawndale. At least 90 percent of the students are expected to be from families living in poverty.

MEANWHILE, DISTRICT OFFICIALS ARE TRYING to address the city's burgeoning Latino population in a revision of a 1981 consent decree

settling a complaint of racial discrimination. Since 1990, the population of Hispanic children in the city has grown by 35 percent, reaching more than 290,000 by 2000. The consent decree requires the district to desegregate its schools by race, integrate its faculty, and make sure that all students have equal educational opportunity, says Joi M. Mecks, a spokeswoman for the school system.

In January 2003, U.S. District Judge Charles P. Kocoras said the consent decree was no longer viable—particularly given how the

Lorenzo Infante, a 7th grader, plays with a pet turtle while his mother, Linda Sarate, looks on. She took part in a 19-day hunger strike in 2001 to press for a new high school in the neighborhood, and hopes her son will be in its 9th grade class when it opens in the fall of 2005.

Ingrid Zuniga, in red, and Itzel Linares shop for sweets at the Dulcelandia, or Candyland, store on 26th Street in the heart of Little Village.

demographics of the schools had changed. He asked the school system to craft a new desegregation plan, and in November, the district and the U.S. Department of Justice did so. The court approved the plan last week.

The modifications to the 1981 consent decree that focus on Latinos include the expansion and increased monitoring of bilingual education programs, according to M. Beatriz Arias, an associate professor of education at Arizona State University in Tempe. She was a consultant for the plan.

As Chicago's Latino population has grown, Latinos have gradually moved into important political positions. In 1983, the City Council had only one alderman who was Latino; today, eight of the 50 aldermen are Latino. Mayor Richard M. Daley appointed Gery Chico, a Mexican-American who was then a top aide, as the president of the board of education when the mayor assumed control of the school system in 1995. Chico stepped down in 2001.

Latino politicians have helped to improve educational opportunities for Latino children, says Ricardo Muñoz, a Mexican-American who since 1993 has been the alderman for Little Village and North Lawndale. "As Latinos began to have more influence and power," he says, "it framed the debate differently, from 'Where are my children being bused?' to 'Why don't I have buildings in my neighborhood?' "

Muñoz says that Latino politicians urged the city to come up with ways to raise the money to build five elementary schools in Little Village in the mid-1990s. Still on the agenda for improving the schooling of Latinos in Chicago is an effort to pressure Illinois legislators to reduce the district's dependence on property taxes, says Muñoz.

A Long Struggle for Equality

Like African-Americans, Mexican-Americans have fought hard for desegregated schools and equal access to education in the United States. As far back as the 1930s, Mexican-Americans living in the Southwest were typically assigned to separate, inferior schools simply because they had Spanish surnames.

The history of the Mexican-American struggle for high-quality schooling is summarized in a soon-to-be-published research paper by M. Beatriz Arias, an associate professor of education at Arizona State University in Tempe.

In 1945, five Mexican-American fathers, including Gonzalo Mendez, filed a class action in a federal court in Los Angeles challenging segregated schools on behalf of their children and 5,000 other Latino children. The judge ruled in favor of the plaintiffs in 1946, and the case was upheld by a federal court of appeals a year later.

The ruling in *Mendez* v. *Westminster School District* was significant, according to Arias, because it was the first decision by a federal court finding that segregation of Mexican-American students was a violation of the 14th Amendment to the U.S. Constitution. The ruling, however, only applied to several districts in California.

Less than a decade later, in 1954, the U.S. Supreme Court decided *Brown* v. *Board of Education of Topeka*. But for years, the ruling was applied only to black students. It wasn't until 1973 that Latinos were recognized in a school desegregation case as a distinct legal class that had experienced discrimination and had the same rights as African-American students to attend desegregated schools. That happened in *Keyes* v. *School District No. 1*, involving the Denver public schools.

As national demographics have changed, Arias says, more school systems are looking for ways to correct past educational discrimination against Latinos. She cites the work by the Chicago school system to strengthen support for Latinos in revising its 1981 desegregation plan, for which she served as a consultant.

Patricia Gándara, a professor of education at the University of California, Davis, argues that the *Brown* decision also laid the groundwork for the 1974 ruling by the Supreme Court in *Lau* v. *Nichols*, which has benefited millions of Latinos.

That ruling required schools, for the first time, to provide extra assistance for students who were learning English so that they could understand the curriculum. The plaintiffs were Chinese-speaking, but the ruling also applied to other language-minority students in the nation.
—MARY ANN ZEHR

"We lose so many of our students after 8th grade," says Carlos Azcoitia, a principal. "We have to do something."

Little Village residents are concentrating on how to make their new high school more successful than the comprehensive high schools now serving large numbers of Hispanic students. Their hopes are riding on a plan to design four separate small schools within the building. Each will have its own principal and academic theme: social justice; world languages; fine and performing arts; and mathematics, science, and technology.

The Little Village CDC has been promised a four-year, $400,000 grant from the Bill & Melinda Gates Foundation, channeled through the Washington-based National Council of La Raza, to help carry out the small-schools concept. The Gates Foundation largely has paid for an additional $75,000 that will be channeled to the community-development corporation through an initiative of the Chicago Community Trust.

Residents want the school to provide a sharp contrast to Little Village's only existing high school, 2,500-student David G. Farragut Career Academy High School. Students who attend Farragut say frequent fistfights in the school are a problem. African-Americans clash with Mexican-American students, and members of Mexican-American gangs also fight with each other, the students say.

Luis Reyes, a 17-year-old who attends Farragut High, says the school has a police substation and lots of security guards, but fights still break out. On a recent winter day, for instance, when classes were scheduled for only a half-day, some students started a fight. A classroom lockdown was ordered, Reyes says, and all students were stuck for an hour and a half.

Farragut offers some good academic programs, such as calculus and physics for college credit, says Reyes. But at the same time, he says, the school is crowded and suffers from high teacher turnover.

More than a quarter of the teachers at Farragut have emergency or provisional credentials; on average, schools in Chicago have 8.2 percent of teachers in the same situation, according to the Illinois School Report Card.

Edward Guerra, Farragut's principal, doesn't think the school is overcrowded, and he says he's had to fire a lot of teachers "for not doing their job."

He names numerous programs he believes are top-notch, including carpentry and a Junior ROTC program with 350 students that operates as a self-contained school. Since he became the principal in the 1994-95 school year, the proportion of students at Farragut who are proficient in reading has tripled, from 7 percent to 21 percent, the student-attendance rate has increased from 70 percent to 92 percent, and enrollment has doubled, says Guerra. He also asserts that safety has improved.

THE BELIEF THAT LATINO YOUTHS in Chicago will be better served by small schools is growing.

Carlos Azcoitia, a Cuban-American who was for the past few years a central-office administrator for the district, returned this school year to his former job as the principal of John Spry Elementary School in Little Village. Under Azcoitia's leadership, the 1,000-student preK-8 school will add high school grades drawing students from the attendance area around it. This school year, Azcoitia added a 9th grade of 32 students. Eventually, the high school will include 100 students, he says.

Already, the results are encouraging, in that the 9th graders have a 98 percent attendance rate, Azcoitia says. He attributes the high rate to the special attention that students receive in small schools, and he hopes the model will catch on with other K-8 schools serving Latinos in Chicago and nationwide. "We lose so many of our students after 8th grade," he says. "We have to do something."

Diego Galeana, 17, who dropped out of Farragut High, says that in his case, attending such a large school was a disaster. He says he was expelled because he had too many absences and tended to get into trouble. Galeana landed a factory job, but he quit after only three weeks. "I was lifting heavy stuff and I'm puny. I said, 'F—- this, I don't like being treated like a Mexican.' "

He joined an activist youth group and became friends with an adult who helped him get placed at the Instituto del Progreso Latino, an alternative public charter school with 60 students in the Mexican-American neighborhood of Pilsen, just east of Little Village. Galeana is still in the 9th grade, which he says is really discouraging, but he's managing much better than he did at Farragut.

"I'm able to solve my problems and not wait a long time," he says.

SOME STUDENTS AND PARENTS IN LITTLE VILLAGE are reluctant to criticize the schools in the neighborhood. "There are no bad schools if the students want to learn," says Rosa Marina in Spanish after dropping off her 6th grade daughter at Spry on a recent winter day. Like many immigrants to Little Village, she and her husband, a factory worker, received only a primary education in Mexico.

But others are critical of the schools, noting that the achievement levels at Farragut and the elementary schools in Little Village are low. In fact, while the test scores of each of the neighborhood's 17 schools, including Farragut, are lower than the average scores for schools in Illinois, five elementary schools in Little Village have test scores that are above-average for the Chicago district. Juan Carlos Alvizar, 18, who lives in Little Village and now goes to the same alternative school as Galeana, recalls that his elementary school in Little Village often got textbooks and computers handed down from other schools. It gave him the feeling that "they're putting you down—like you're not going to be anything," he says.

Residents of Little Village say they want their children to get a good education so they can do well in American society.

At Farragut High, which serves the Little Village neighborhood, six security guards and a police substation keep order among 2,500 students.

"Education is everything," says Sarate, the hunger-striker. "I didn't have a good one." She attended a school in Chicago for students with disabilities because she had polio as a child. During the hunger strike, she fasted until she could barely hold her head up. Sarate expects to enroll her son Lorenzo Infante, now a 7th grader, in the new high school, and is confident he'll get a good education there.

De Leon of the Little Village CDC believes that community involvement is going to make the difference in the new high school's effectiveness for Latino students. But as a middle-class Mexican-American resident of Little Village and a college graduate who went to Roman Catholic schools, he acknowledges that he isn't yet confident that Little Village's public schools will be good enough for his own daughter, Lucia, who is now an infant.

"I would like to be able to send her to a public school," he says. "I'm conflicted." ■

Arlington, Va., offers a case study of the promise and challenges facing a diverse public school system.

In High School, Race Is a Subtext

Do issues of race and ethnic origin matter to young people in 2004, 50 years after the U.S. Supreme Court issued its ruling in *Brown* v. *Board of Education of Topeka* outlawing segregated public schools?

At Wakefield High School in Arlington, Va., racial and ethnic diversity is part of the fabric of life. Students from a wide array of backgrounds sit together in class, eat lunch together, and play sports together.

Half a century ago, such scenes would have been unimaginable. Wakefield High was a segregated school serving only whites. And residents of the Northern Virginia suburb of Washington burned crosses to show their hostility toward integration.

Today, Wakefield is making a major push to help minority students reach their full potential

Sayola Delgado, a student at Wakefield High School in Arlington, Va., stops at her locker between classes. Teenagers at the highly diverse school often come together across racial and ethnic lines, but pull apart at other times.

Allison Shelley

academically, including an emphasis on enrolling them in Advanced Placement classes.

But there are still miles to go. Teenagers at the school are so comfortable with diversity that many claim to be colorblind. The truth about race for Wakefield's students, like many young people across the nation, is not so simple, though. The messages they end up sending—and receiving—are mixed.

Sophomore Hina Munir, center, eats lunch in the school cafeteria with a group of her friends.
The girls, whose families are from India and Pakistan, speak Hindi and Urdu when they get together.

Mixed Messages

Do issues of race and ethnic origin matter to young people in 2004? Students at the highly diverse Wakefield High School in Arlington, Va., say no—and yes. Very much.

Two Wakefield High students share a private moment.

FACES FROM THE PAST

A yearbook page with members of the senior class at Wakefield High School in Arlington, Va., in 1956 shows an all-white lineup of students. Before 1963, the school was segregated.

Arlington, Va.

I t's 10 minutes into lunch at Wakefield High School, and the cafeteria is crowded and smelling of french fries. At a long, narrow table in the middle of the room, four girls set down their trays. Chatting in Spanish about classes and boyfriends, they lean close to one another to hear over the din.

Over near the big window, a white boy and a black boy laugh and poke each other, knocking their crumpled brown lunch bags to the floor. An Asian girl and a Latino boy wait silently in the lunch line together, her head on his shoulder, his arm around her waist.

This scene would have been impossible here 50 years ago, as the U.S. Supreme Court prepared to hand down its decision in *Brown* v. *Board of Education of Topeka,* outlawing systems of racially segregated public schools. Back then, every student in this cafeteria was white, a truly bizarre notion to these teenagers so accustomed to racial and ethnic diversity.

But as colorblind as these young people claim to be, as comfortable as many are with a rich cross-racial and cross-ethnic mixture, the truth about race in this close-in Virginia suburb of Washington, a half-century after *Brown*, is double-edged. In some ways, it doesn't matter at all. And in many others, it matters. A lot.

It shows up in the way students map out the

BY CATHERINE GEWERTZ

Photographs by Allison Shelley

social terrain of the cafeteria.

"Lots of times, kids hang with their own race 'cause it's more comfortable," Calvin Height, 17, an African-American student sporting a closely trimmed goatee, says as he surveys the vast room. "But it can also be what you're into, you know, like those guys over there"—he points to two tables of students, all black—"they're into rap music."

Alfred Simkin, a lanky, white 17-year-old, says some kids sit together because they're obsessed with a certain popular card game, and others because they love to skateboard. The friends at his table—all white—share a love of rock music. "Over there, that's the Asian table, and those tables over there," Simkin says, gesturing toward the center of the room, "usually have a lot of the kids who talk Spanish."

These students, who have no idea that opponents of school integration once burned crosses in this community, are quick to say that race and ethnic origin have little meaning in their lives at Wakefield High.

But almost immediately, they proceed to spin out stories showing that their ancestry runs like theme music through their days, sounding notes of pride, guilt, confusion, and anger; playing at some moments almost inaudibly, and at others, painfully loudly.

BEYOND THE WALLS OF WAKEFIELD high school, race and ethnicity have carved clear patterns throughout the 19,000-student Arlington school district. The busing that sought to even the distribution of black and white children in the schools here ended more than a decade ago, allowing housing patterns—wealthier, white families in north Arlington, lower-income black and Hispanic families in the

School counselor Al Reid, left, shares a pizza with seniors Christopher Ward, middle, and Jaime Quinteros. The students are members of a support group that was formed to encourage black and Hispanic boys to take advanced classes and to help them succeed once enrolled.

south, Asian families scattered more evenly throughout—to be replicated in the schools.

At Wakefield, the southernmost of Arlington's three high schools, the enrollment is 46 percent Hispanic, 27 percent African-American, 16 percent white, and 11 percent Asian or Pacific Islander. Nearly half the students qualify for subsidized school meals. Yorktown, the northernmost high school, is 66 percent white, 17 percent Hispanic, 11 percent Asian, and 7 percent black. Only 16 percent of its students qualify for reduced-price meals.

Wakefield trails the other two high schools on state and college-entrance tests, and enrolls fewer students in advanced coursework. Districtwide, racial and ethnic achievement gaps persist, as white and Asian students outpace their black and Latino peers.

Those patterns have led Arlington administrators to focus unusually sharply on

enabling black and Latino students to flourish. To accomplish that, they see pressure on two levers as key: preparing students for challenging work, and preparing teachers to engage them in it effectively. Neither lever will work, district leaders contend, unless teachers know how to build caring relationships with students.

"The focus is on the quality of the experiences kids get in the classroom," says Robert G. Smith, the sandy-haired, bespectacled superintendent who has made closing the skills gaps between racial and ethnic groups a top priority in his six years in Arlington. "It goes beyond saying, 'All kids can learn.' It's the expectations we set for them, the access to opportunities that we give them. It's the messages teachers convey in class through their interactions, that they *can do this*."

"That relationship piece is make-or-break,"

says Cheryl Robinson, the district's minority-achievement coordinator. "If you can't connect with the kids, all the other stuff is moot."

Arlington's approach seems to be yielding results. Since 1999, students in all racial and ethnic groups have been scoring better on statewide tests, and the gaps between groups are narrowing.

The persistence of disparities means that much remains to be done, however. District leaders know those differences arise from a tangle of many threads, from adults' low expectations and poor teaching to socioeconomic pressure, the influence of pop culture, and complex family, peer, and cultural dynamics.

But in a district that is financially fortunate, unified by a clear mission, and small enough to get the message out, closing the gap is seen as a manageable goal.

"If anyone could close the achievement gap, it would be a district like us," says Kathleen F. Grove, the assistant superintendent for instruction. "I believe there are answers, and we can figure out what to do. I'm not frustrated …" she says, pausing for a smile, " … yet. If we stop making progress, then I'll be concerned."

SAMANTHA HO, 17, WHOSE PARENTS ARE CHINESE and Vietnamese, is sick of the misplaced beliefs she has to combat in her fellow Wakefield High students every week. "There's always this assumption that you can't speak English," she says with a frustrated eye roll. "People are like, 'Can you understand me?' and I'm like, 'Uhhh, yeahhh, I was born here.' It hurts."

"Yeah, I'm from the Philippines, and this Indian girl asks me if I'm Chinese," says Domicyl Cadag, 16. "People are always asking us if we are Chinese."

These girls and other members of Wakefield's Asian students' club, meeting in a classroom after school one day last month, begin reeling off the assumptions that other students often make about them: Good at math. Smart. Quiet. Disciplined. Not good at sports. The teenagers laugh uncomfortably.

"I kind of feel offended that they know so little about us," says Mary Jane Riguera, 15, who is Filipino-American.

They are not alone in the slights they experience at the hands of their classmates. Stories abound of insensitive comments, often laden with stereotypes.

"If I had a dollar for every time someone asked me if I play basketball," Nahid Koohkanrizi, 17, a tall African-American student who is the treasurer of Wakefield's student government association, says during a break in a recent meeting of the group.

Senior Paul Morales, left, who is from Bolivia, plays chess against senior Hernan Lamas, from Argentina, in the school's media center during a class period.

41

Many students at Wakefield say their peers pressure them to socialize only with teenagers of their own racial or ethnic group.

Many students experience pressure to socialize only with teenagers of their own racial or ethnic group.

"I hang out with mostly Asian kids, and [African-American] kids have come up to me and said, 'It's wrong for you to hang out with them instead of with us," says Destynie DuMar, 16, who is multiracial.

Wakefield's many immigrant students grapple not only with their peers' stereotypes and ignorance of their cultures, but also with language difficulties that can make them shy in the classroom and family pressures that can complicate school life. Many of their parents, unfamiliar with the American education system, don't understand how they can be advocates for their children.

Dina Ascencio, 18, who arrived from El Salvador five years ago, says she can't be involved in many after-school activities because her father, worried by the many stories he has heard about freewheeling American teenagers, fears she could get into trouble. He refused to let his daughter go on an overnight trip to college campuses, organized by school counselors, until one of Wakefield's bilingual resource assistants called and explained how valuable the trip could be for his daughter.

Claudia Torres feels the dual pressure of succeeding both as an American and a Peruvian. "I have to speak as clear English as they do, and show everyone I can do it, and I

Krysta Roa, a junior from Indonesia, right, and Xiang He, a sophomore from China, chat during a physical education class.

have to be the perfect Peruvian, too," says the petite 17-year-old. "You have to be like a bridge, teaching your parents about American culture, and teaching your friends about Peruvian culture.

"It gets tiring. Can't I just be normal?"

Down a long hallway and around the corner on another afternoon, members of a journalism class share widely varying analyses of the role race plays in their lives.

"We've been brought up in a melting pot with so many cultures here, so diversity is second nature to us," says Alex LaPiana, 17, a white student who is the editor of the student newspaper. Veronica Rios, 17, says she thinks

everybody gets along at Wakefield, and as a Latina, sees herself with extra opportunity—such as college scholarships—rather than as a member of a disadvantaged group.

Some of their classmates see it differently.

"They way I talk, black kids are always telling me, 'Oh, she talks so proper, she must think she's white,' " says Hadiatu Sumah, 16, whose parents are West African. "Hispanic and white kids accept me more than black kids do."

John Stephens, 16, says that he and other African-American males sense that others "expect us to have this gangster image goin' on. I've seen some really smart people act dumber than they are because that's what's expected."

EXPECTATIONS TAINTED BY CULTURAL IGNORANCE and bias too often seep into adults and the children they teach, and influence classroom learning, say experts in the field. Dynamics like those are on the demolition schedule at the Friday pizza lunches of a Wakefield High group called "the cohort."

Formed four years ago to combat the virtual absence of black and Latino males in Advanced Placement classes, the group tackles head-on the academic, social, and emotional issues that can

Sophomore Amber Taylor has her hair braided by freshman Yvauhn Curtis after classes end for the day.

Adults are largely to blame for making race an issue, many teenagers charge. What they want, they say, is to be themselves.

hinder high achievement.

With their adult advisers, the young men bond and problem-solve on an outdoor ropes course. They expand their horizons on overnight trips to college campuses and share the trials of applying. They learn to advocate for themselves in high-level classes, and to manage frustration when the going gets rough.

And over weekly pizza, they talk about everything from the responsibilities of manhood to the need for support in staying on a productive path.

"I'd be kind of lost without the cohort," says Sergio Padilla, a soft-spoken 16-year-old from Bolivia. "Some of my friends, they don't set goals. They don't care about going to college. I want to go, but it seemed scary to figure it out. In the cohort, I found out a lot about college and financial aid."

Chris Ward, 17, who is African-American, says the cohort helps him withstand the pressure from friends to goof off.

"Here, you keep your eyes focused on the prize," he says. "When you do good, these people are not going to laugh at you. They're going to give you a pat on the back. And when you're not doing well, they're going to tell you to step it up."

The cohort has grown from 15 juniors and seniors in 2000 to 77 in all four grades this year. It has more than tripled the number of black and Latino males in AP classes over the past three years. Wakefield is expanding the program next year, so that any student who wants to take

an AP class may do so, with support groups that impart skills such as how to take good notes, set up a study group, or tackle college-level texts.

Alan Beitler, a school social worker who is one of three advisers to the cohort, says its success is based on helping young men overcome self-doubt fueled by the stereotypes and low expectations around them. Instead, they learn that they have great potential and adults rooting for them.

"We look past the grades, past the behavior, past the dress. That isn't the essential part of them," says Beitler, a bearded former minister in jeans and a leather jacket. "I want to teach them that I believe in them, and that they can, also."

IN A BASEMENT ROOM ONE WINTER DAY after school, 11 Wakefield teachers are examining their own practices to uncover biases and weaknesses, particularly in their interactions with low-achieving students. Led by Robinson, the district's minority-achievement coordinator, they learn how to better ask students probing questions, listen carefully to answers, and make emotional connections, using touch or eye contact.

Teachers in this training allow their colleagues to observe them in the classroom, marking down on clipboards any differences in how they manage low-achieving and high-achieving students. Later, they receive feedback. Do they ask struggling students questions that

demand higher-order thinking, or mostly simple yes-or-no questions? Do they "connect" better with the high-achieving students? Are they quicker to become angry with low achievers?

In the classrooms along Wakefield's long hallways, teachers—most of whom are non-Hispanic and white—vary in their awareness of those dynamics, and their openness to considering them.

Doug Burns, a slightly built English teacher with an intense blue-eyed gaze, says that the curriculum is full of cultural bias. He needs to serve as a bridge to make it relevant for his students, who come with a myriad of cultural and religious beliefs and experiences, he says. He'll do "whatever it takes" to reach them, and show them that "you and I are a team, and it's time for us to get to work."

Many teachers embrace the students' diversity as an enriching facet of Wakefield life, and students at the school almost universally say their teachers have high expectations for them. A few teachers, though, express doubts that all students are able or properly prepared to navigate the high-level courses.

"Sometimes a particular goal might not suit a particular student," says one teacher, who asked not to be named for fear of appearing uncooperative with the school's priorities.

Some teachers struggle with the challenge of tuning in to each student's needs, and say that the pressure to prepare them to perform well on statewide tests makes doing that even tougher.

Some are not at ease with the idea that they should try to "read" students, so they might understand, for instance, that a student who seems tuned out might just be in need of encouragement.

Physics teacher Jim Chalker, who at 49 describes himself as a "curmudgeon," acknowledges that he "should be better" about varying his teaching techniques to suit students' needs.

"I tend to engage the ones who are having trouble but trying, and not as much the ones who aren't interested," he says. "I know I've dropped the ball with some students, but I have enough things in my head that I can't stop and say about each kid, 'What does he need?' "

Shortly before leaving Wakefield High to move to the Midwest recently, Chalker, who is white, reflected on his experiences with his array of students. Black students, he says, have been "louder" in his classes. And it's mostly the black students, he says, who turn their backs and walk away from him when he tries to talk to them about their hallway behavior.

"I admit I may have some prejudices," he says. "They've probably affected my teaching. I'd like to think they haven't."

TEACHERS' ATTITUDES HAVE LEFT A TRAIL OF STORIES to tell for Tiffany Ratliff, André Baker, and Brandon Day. Leaders of black students' groups at Wakefield, all three recall being screened for special education classes at least once earlier in their school careers. In all cases, their parents intervened, ensuring their placement in regular or high-level classes.

"They label you at a young age," says Ratliff, 17,

Members of the crew team work out in the basement before heading to the Anacostia River for a rowing session after school.

a tall, restless girl with dozens of tiny braids.

"Yeah, people see you're a black kid and figure they ought to be prepared for the worst," says Baker, a round-faced, talkative 17-year-old.

He recalled one time a few years ago, while he was attending another school, when he argued heatedly with something his white teacher said. She sent him to the principal's office, saying she was afraid he was going to hit her.

"I'm all loud, and I'm in baggy clothes, and I do like this," Baker says, gesturing broadly with his arms, "and they say I'm 'ghetto,' and

that's it for me."

These teenagers, and many others, say adults are largely to blame for making race an issue. College applications ask them their race. Guest speakers at school deliberately provoke debate about race. Adults at home tease that they should never date someone of another race. All they want, many students say, is just to be allowed to be themselves.

"People keep talking and talking about race this, and race that," says Ratliff, "and I just keep thinking, why should it matter?" ■

Parental choice, a strategy once used to help integrate schools via magnets and special programs, is now under fire as increasing racial separation.

School Choice and the Legacy of *Brown*

Even before segregated schooling was struck down a half-century ago, the issue of school choice was a theme running through America's desegregation struggle.

By bringing their cause to court, black families rebelled against being denied the choice of attending better-equipped schools reserved for whites.

When ordered to desegregate, many communities on paper gave blacks the "freedom of choice" to go to white schools—but, in practice, made most of them stay put.

Many whites exercised choice by leaving for private schools or the suburbs, even as policymakers set up magnet schools to bring the races together through the power of choice.

Some 35 years after the U.S. Supreme Court issued its 1954 ruling in *Brown* v. *Board of*

Tammy Malone, a 5th grader who attends Garden Homes Lutheran School in Milwaukee with a voucher, finishes an assignment before heading out for recess. Supporters see vouchers as an outgrowth of the drive for equal opportunity. Others strongly disagree.

Allison Shelley

Education of Topeka, African-American activists' discontent over their school choices in the era of busing helped give rise to the voucher movement in Milwaukee.

Are publicly financed tuition vouchers for children from low-income families a new twist on African-Americans' long march for equal educational opportunity? Ask people in Milwaukee, the birthplace of the voucher movement, and you'll get different answers.

Marquis Coulter, a 9th grader who attends Messmer High School in Milwaukee with a state-financed voucher, takes part in a voluntary prayer service offered during lunchtime at the Roman Catholic school.

Hearts and Minds

In the bitter policy battles over publicly financed tuition vouchers, both opponents and supporters lay claim to the legacy of the *Brown* decision.

Howard L. Fuller, a former superintendent of the Milwaukee public schools, has become a leading national advocate of school choice.

Sherman Gessert/Milwaukee Journal

A NEW DAY

A Milwaukee principal greets new students as they get off the bus at her school on Sept. 7, 1976, the first day of busing under the desegregation plan for the Milwaukee public schools.

Milwaukee

As the U.S. Supreme Court's historic ruling *Brown* v. *Board of Education of Topeka* turns 50 this week, don't expect Annette P. Williams to be wishing it a happy anniversary. After all, it was her disillusionment with school desegregation that stirred her to lead the charge 14 years ago for this city's pioneering program of private school vouchers.

Not that Williams, who has represented a slice of inner-city Milwaukee in the Wisconsin legislature for 24 of her 67 years, was a great fan of the legally sanctioned segregation that was struck down by *Brown*. But the one-time welfare mother saw the approach local leaders took to bringing the races together—mainly busing black children to faraway neighborhoods—as an unmitigated disaster for the black community she still represents.

"Desegregation is about the movement of bodies; it had nothing to do with education," asserts Williams, who goes by her middle name, Polly. "Our focus in the Milwaukee Parental Choice Program is all about education. It's not about integration or desegregation. We don't even think about that."

Given the demographic reality of Milwaukee today, such views are understandable. With white students down to a small minority—not just in public schools, but in many private ones as well— one-race schools are far easier to find than

BY CAROLINE HENDRIE

Photographs by
Allison Shelley

Yvonne Ali, the founder of the Agape Center of Academic Excellence, in black jacket, and Annette "Polly" Williams, an early backer of vouchers, stand outside a theater purchased by the school.

examples of multicultural mixing in Wisconsin's largest city. Yet the ghosts of desegregation battles past still linger in the movement Williams helped kick-start here on Lake Michigan's western shore. References to *Brown*—and the epic struggle by African-Americans for educational justice that it symbolizes—have become common not only here, but virtually anywhere that the contentious issue of private school choice is on the agenda. Leaders on both sides of the voucher divide are invoking the landmark case to promote their visions, not just in legal skirmishes and policy blueprints, but also in the battle for hearts and minds.

"Both sides use the same language of equality and opportunity," says John C. Brittain, a law professor at Texas Southern University in Houston who represented the plaintiffs in a long-running desegregation case in Hartford, Conn.

Behind the words are challenges to rethink old questions about the most promising strategies for achieving the long-cherished goal of equal educational opportunity in America. At stake for both camps is the right to carry the torch of *Brown*—to lay claim to the dream of a nation where skin color plays no role in a child's shot at success.

PREACHING TO A CHOIR OF SCHOOL CHOICE ACTIVISTS here a couple of months ago, U.S. Secretary of Education Rod Paige noted that a half-century after the *Brown* ruling, the problems faced by black children "are still there to see: lack of educational achievement, the denial of educational opportunities, and the economic consequences that follow." The Mississippi native then reached back further—back to the 19th-century fight to end slavery.

Howard Fuller worries that "the war" over vouchers has divided people who should be working together to improve the schools.

"In my view, opportunity scholarships provide a workable, hopeful alternative to open private schools to low-income and minority students," he said of vouchers in his March 5 speech at the annual meeting of the Washington-based Black Alliance for Educational Options. "For each of these students, this is educational emancipation."

Another son of the segregated South, Supreme Court Justice Clarence Thomas, sounded a similar theme in his concurring opinion in the high court's 5-4 decision upholding the Cleveland voucher program in 2002. "Today many of our inner-city public schools deny emancipation to urban minority students," he wrote. "Despite this court's observation nearly 50 years ago in *Brown* v. *Board of Education* that it is doubtful that any child may reasonably be expected to succeed in life if he is denied the opportunity of an education, urban children have been forced into a system that continually fails them."

And during last year's bitter debate in Congress over the soon-to-start voucher program for the District of Columbia, parent activists mounted an ad campaign that went so far as to liken voucher foes to Southern segregationists. In a TV spot targeting Sen. Edward M. Kennedy, D-Mass., for example, the leader of the parents' group recalled being reassured by her mother that the late Sen. Robert F. Kennedy was fighting against those who sought to "stop our race from getting a good education." Photographs of such champions of segregation as Alabama

Gov. George C. Wallace flashed on the screen.

"Senator Kennedy, your brothers fought for us," Virginia Walden-Ford, an African-American mother who heads the group D.C. Parents for School Choice, said in the spot. "Why do you fight against us?"

National opponents of vouchers were outraged by the ads. In Milwaukee, local leaders of the National Association for the Advancement of Colored People also take issue with the portrayal of vouchers as a modern-day civil rights cause.

"We don't feel that going the way of vouchers complements *Brown* v. *Board of Education*, because it lends itself toward segregation more than anything else," says Jerry Ann Hamilton, the president of the Milwaukee chapter of the NAACP. "The education system has to be revamped, but we think that going the way of vouchers is leading away from what we had in mind."

Paulette Y. Copeland, a member of the board of the local NAACP chapter and the vice president of the Milwaukee Teachers Education Association, also is rankled by suggestions that vouchers are a means of addressing the unfulfilled promises of *Brown*. Copeland, a literacy specialist for the Milwaukee school district, rejects the argument that vouchers help emancipate poor families by giving them the same type of choices that wealthier families have long enjoyed. "Choice schools are not the same quality as those schools open to the middle-class and rich families," she contends.

Still, to address social-justice concerns, Copeland suggests that foundations and wealthy individuals that back voucher-advocacy efforts instead give tuition aid directly to low-income families. "Let the public schools deal with the public money," she says.

MILWAUKEE'S VOUCHER PROGRAM HAS MUSHROOMED from serving 341 students at seven secular private schools in 1990 to supporting 13,231 students in 112 schools, 79 of them religious. The $76 million program has always been limited to children from families within the city limits whose incomes do not exceed 175 percent of the federal poverty level, or about $32,500 for a family of four. In practical terms, that means that the program is open mainly to children of color, a majority of them black.

Among the schools spawned by the choice program is the Milwaukee Multicultural Academy, located in a mainly black neighborhood on the city's north side. Housed in a former synagogue, the school proudly posts its mission at the door: "Developing the Multicultural Mind for the New Millennium."

But inside the worn-looking, one-story structure, the scene is far less multicultural than Principal Jerry D. Fair would like. When he started the school with 27 students six years ago, Fair was hoping to replicate the racial and ethnic diversity of two public schools in the city that he

Students at the Agape Center of Academic Excellence learn in classrooms set up to resemble living rooms.

once headed. "I had this multicultural vision," he says between interruptions in his cramped office.

As it's turned out, all but three of his 131 students are black. Many students arrive years behind academically. Seven of the 12 new 5th graders he accepted this year tested at a prekindergarten reading level, he says. As the president of an association of black-run independent schools in Milwaukee, Fair is committed to strengthening schools run by and for African-Americans. Yet he hopes to move his school someday to a less homogeneous neighborhood, so his multicultural vision could be realized. "Diversity is just really an important thing for me," he says.

From the start of the choice program, opponents have complained that it would worsen school segregation in a city long divided by race. The NAACP made such a prediction, for example, in a lawsuit that unsuccessfully challenged the 1995 state law that expanded the program to religious schools.

A 2002 study by Howard L. Fuller, a former Milwaukee superintendent who is now a leading national advocate of school choice, found that compared with students in the city's public schools, a slightly lower percentage of youngsters in voucher schools in 2001-02 were in "racially isolated" settings. The difference was small, though, with 49.8 percent of students in the participating private schools in such settings—defined as having at least 90 percent either minority or white enrollment—compared with 54.4 percent in public schools. In general, the study said, students in participating religious schools were less likely to be racially isolated than in the secular schools, many of which are all-black or nearly so.

"[T]he data suggest that including religious

Paulette Y. Copeland, the vice president of the Milwaukee Teachers Education Association, rejects the argument that vouchers emancipate poor families. Schools participating in the voucher program, she argues, aren't of the same quality as those open to middle-class and wealthy families.

schools in a voucher program targeting low-income families has contributed to more integration in private religious schools than in the Milwaukee public school system," says the analysis co-written by Fuller, who is now a professor at Marquette University here.

Critics of the choice program are skeptical of such conclusions. Jennifer Morales, an outspoken voucher opponent on the Milwaukee school board, dismisses the numbers as "ridiculous." "The private schools are not integrated," she says. "I don't think they're any more integrated than we are."

Whether or not that's true, says Fuller, discussions of racial balancing in the schools have been made moot in his hometown by the steady decline in the white population. In the 105,000-student Milwaukee public schools, just 15 percent of students were white as of 2002-03, down from 26 percent a decade earlier. Sixty percent were black; 17 percent were Hispanic, up from 10 percent a decade earlier. Statistics on the demographic breakdown of participants in the

voucher program are not available.

"While integration is still the ultimate goal, the reality for most black students in inner-city America is that they're not going to be in integrated schools," Fuller says. "So the question is, how are they going to be educated?"

THE REV. E. ALLEN SORUM, A WHITE LUTHERAN MINISTER whose church runs a school in a north-side neighborhood that has become nearly all black, offers one answer to that question. The school's enrollment has shifted to the point that the only white students for the past 15 years have been children of school staff members. But despite the lack of integration, Sorum sees his school as dispensing tools youngsters can use to break down racial barriers later in life.

"The world is racist," he tells the 110-student school's combined 7th and 8th grade class during a recent discussion of the voucher program. "But God's given you great gifts so you can make God look good in the world. If you're a highly educated,

In Milwaukee, dissatisfaction with the results of busing helped fuel the support for vouchers among black parents and policymakers.

God-loving, righteous-preaching Christian, you're going to dispel whatever prejudices other races have when you go out into society."

Without the $5,882 tuition vouchers that the state-run program provides, Sorum figures that Garden Homes Lutheran School would have shut down two years ago. Instead, the school is on a growth spurt that will quicken next year, when it moves across the street into a new facility being added onto the church. At that point, the old school building will be turned over to a Montessori public school that now occupies two classrooms in the building.

That arrangement is part of an unusual partnership Sorum has forged with public school educators not only to share space, but also to work jointly to promote the educational options in their neighborhood. Door to door and on street corners, they hand out brochures promoting the "Garden Homes Community of Schools"—the Lutheran school, the Montessori program, and a public elementary school, as well as a public high school and a Baptist one. The goal, Sorum says, is to serve families and build up the community.

The promotion is needed in part because of the legacy of desegregation, says Kenneth Johnson, a member of the Milwaukee school board who represents the Garden Homes neighborhood. "We have 30 years of conditioning saying the school in your neighborhood is no good," says Johnson, a supporter both of the voucher program and of a neighborhood schools initiative that the district started in 2000 to

reduce busing. "That's so misguided."

Terry McKissick, the African-American principal of the nearby Garden Homes Community School, has canvassed the neighborhood with Sorum to talk up his 350-student public elementary school, in the hope of eventually reaching his 500-pupil enrollment target. "What I can see happening now is going back to the '50s and '60s style of education: Children walk to school, families know each other, and parents participate in school events," McKissick says. "When they brought in busing … you were integrating schools, but you were breaking up communities."

A CORNERSTONE OF VOUCHER CRITICS' ARGUMENT against the choice program is that participating private schools are not required to administer standardized tests or to make the results public. "Rod Paige, the last time he was here, talked about voucher schools helping to close the achievement gap," Copeland says. "We don't know that. We have no idea if the children in these schools are learning anything, because they're not accountable."

Don't try telling that to Yvonne Ali, the founder and executive director of the Agape Center of Academic Excellence, a nonprofit organization that runs a child-care center and K-8 school on the north side. Ali's more than 320 students include about 145 children in the voucher program and roughly 175 whom the

school contracts with Milwaukee district to educate. Because of the school's connection to the district, Ali is required to administer the same tests the public schools give. But for both groups, she receives thousands of dollars less per pupil than is spent in the public school system. Ali sees that arrangement as a form of discrimination that is hurting independent, black-run schools such as hers.

"I'm straddling the two worlds, and I'm in an accountability situation that says I must produce," she says. "We're constantly trying to do as much or more as any public school would do, and we still receive less money. It's still separate, but it is not equal."

Still, Ali says she does not think of the vouchers as a civil rights issue, in part because the program was not set up to serve only minority children. Enrollment at her own school is almost all black, but that is because of who chooses to enroll, she says, not by design. "We have some of the opponents of school choice saying that it's still separation—it's for all minority children—which is false," Ali says of the voucher program. "It's for economically deprived children."

POLLY WILLIAMS, THE LEGISLATOR, says poor children and their education have always been her chief concerns. And just as she criticized supporters of desegregation for overlooking such youngsters' best interests, she has begun leveling similar charges against some in the choice

At Garden Homes Lutheran School, a child plays basketball on the concrete lot next to the school used for recess. Without the state money provided by the voucher program, the school likely would have been forced to close, its principal says. Instead, it plans to move across the street next year to a better facility.

movement. She sponsored the bill that extended the voucher program beyond secular schools, and says she doesn't regret it. But she worries that the new facilities popping up at some religious schools around town are signs that the program may be losing its focus.

"This was not intended to be a building program," Williams says. She also contends that religious school leaders and other proponents of choice are seeking legislative adjustments to the program that are "driven more to support the building of new schools as opposed to the needs of the child."

Among them is legislation to lift a cap that limits participation in the choice program to roughly 15 percent of the city's public school enrollment. While many other choice advocates can't understand Williams's stance, she says she views the proposal as a form of tinkering that could spur other changes that would shift the focus beyond city children from low-income households. "The Catholic schools are the ones who want a lot of these changes," she says.

One school pushing to remove the cap is Messmer High School, a Roman Catholic school where most teachers and administrators are white, but whose student enrollment is now 91 percent black. Since Messmer began accepting vouchers in 1998, the school's enrollment has risen from 307 to 545, and the share of youngsters using the tuition aid has grown to 73 percent. Indeed, the choice program has been such a help to the school that its new gymnasium is named the Gov. Tommy G. Thompson Athletic Center, for the former Republican governor of Wisconsin who signed the program into law.

Yet Messmer High Principal Jeff R. Monday says observers are wrong to assume that at Messmer and other religious schools, "the physical expansion is being done with choice money." At his school, he says, the expansion was in the works well before the school entered the program. "Every dime that went into expanding the school facilities was money that was raised privately," he says. "So to say that the school is more concerned with building than kids is absolutely false."

For his part, Fuller says he is saddened by the internecine disputes within Milwaukee's choice community. More important, he is troubled by the bitter rift between voucher supporters and opponents, which he says detracts from the determination that both groups share to continue the work begun by the crusaders against segregated schools.

"If we didn't have to spend so much money, time, and energy on the fight to just exist, we could be using those resources to make the schools better," Fuller says. "There are people on both sides of the issue who should be working together who aren't because of the war. That's the tragedy of the whole thing, but I don't see that changing." ■

Crumbling Legacy

BY JOETTA L. SACK
Photographs by
James W. Prichard

A vision for educating
blacks and bridging
racial divides
is fading from
the landscape

Wake Forest, N.C.

Ravaged by time and neglect, DuBois High School still stands as a symbol of the decent education that African-Americans across the South craved, well before they were allowed into the schools attended by their white peers.

The boarded-up red-brick structure has gaping holes in its roof. Weeds have overtaken much of the sidewalk. Wooden eaves are rotting, and the front entry is sagging sadly after years of indifference.

To the few who know the story of this school, though, its tired appearance can't overshadow the building's dramatic history.

When it was built in 1926, the DuBois school was part of a vision shared by Booker T. Washington and one of the leading white capitalists of the time to build top-notch public schools for African-Americans across

the South, from Texas all the way to Maryland.

Like many of the other historic "Rosenwald schools"—named for the business leader and philanthropist who helped pay to build them—the DuBois school became a beacon for impoverished African-Americans, divided by railroad tracks from the handsome houses and schools of white residents a few blocks away.

Despite the rich history of those schools, their story has been largely ignored. That is beginning to change. Most recently, the impending 50th anniversary of *Brown* v. *Board of Education of Topeka*, the U.S. Supreme Court decision that overturned racial segregation in public schooling, is bringing renewed attention to the schools.

EASTMAN SCHOOL Halifax County, N.C. Students attend one of the state's 787 "Rosenwald schools."

Only in the past 20 years or so have historic preservationists turned their attention to documenting Rosenwald schools, which otherwise have been slowly disintegrating into the landscape, taking the stories—and, often, the pride—of their

MAYFLOWER SCHOOL Inez, N.C.

More than 5,000 Rosenwald schools built with funds from a white philanthropist and opened in the early 1900s for black children not allowed in local public schools. Above, nestled in the middle of a field about a quarter-mile off rural Highway 58, the Mayflower School was one of 15 one-room Rosenwald schools built in Warren County, and is one of the few remaining one-room Rosenwald buildings. Left, old desks and a stove remain in the school, reminders of the site's former life.

Before preservationists can salvage and restore Rosenwald schools, they must first find the often-forgotten buildings.

communities with them.

In the 1970s, preservationists were "basically looking at rich white men's houses," says Claudia R. Brown, the architectural-survey coordinator and an architectural historian with North Carolina's historic-preservation office, located in Raleigh.

"Over time, that has changed dramatically," she adds. More recent surveys of historical buildings have included modest dwellings and other sites, including Rosenwald schools, that tell the stories of average citizens.

More than 5,300 Rosenwald schools and other buildings were built as part of the project from 1913 to 1932, in 15 states. More than 800 of the structures were in North Carolina.

THE IDEA FOR THE SCHOOLS WAS CONCEIVED by the black educator and author Washington and financed by Julius Rosenwald, the president of Sears, Roebuck, and Co., the Chicago-based mail-order giant and department store chain.

Rosenwald set up a program that offered state-of-the-art facility plans designed by architects from Tuskegee Institute and funding for grants that were matched by local communities. The schools served black students who were shut out of regular public schools in the era of Jim Crow, or who attended classes in decrepit structures—if at all.

"To lose these buildings is to lose an important

story and an important chain of history that made *Brown* v. *Board* a more important movement," says John Hildreth, the director of the Southern office, in Charleston, S.C., of the Washington-based National Trust for Historic Preservation.

More important, perhaps, is the desire of the many alumni of Rosenwald schools who want to tell their stories and recapture some of the bonds that held their communities together during the years of segregation.

It's a struggle that will require time, money, and dedication, not unlike the efforts to see the schools themselves built in the early 20th century.

"The challenges that face Rosenwald schools are challenges that are not new to the historic-preservation movement," Hildreth says. "In many cases, [the challenges] are exacerbated in that they are often in rural locations and often have been abandoned from the original use."

Simply finding Rosenwald schools has been a challenge. North Carolina's historians have been using a 1930s list to help them locate the old school sites. But, they've frequently found that the name of a community is wrong, or isn't used anymore, or that the town no longer exists. And the schools could be hidden anywhere in the state's vast rural areas.

Further, the plans for the Rosenwald schools were often reused—so that schools that look like Rosenwald schools, in fact, are not—and it's not always possible to say if a school was Rosenwald-funded.

Because little money is available, Brown, of the North Carolina preservation office, relies on volunteers to conduct surveys that document the buildings.

When an intern in Brown's office tried to find the remaining Rosenwald schools in rural Bertie County, on the North Carolina coast,

PRINCETON GRADED SCHOOL
Princeton, N.C.

This brick school was unusual because its auditorium had stationary seating. Currently up for sale, it is occasionally used for community events, such as a yard sale last summer. An abandoned piano, far left, sits in an empty classroom. Other items are strewn about the school, including leftovers from the yard sale.

A Mutual Concern

In the early 1900s, multimillionaire Julius Rosenwald decided to use his personal riches to help better the lives of blacks in the South.

Rosenwald, the president of Sears, Roebuck, and Co., befriended Booker T. Washington, the founder of Tuskegee Institute in Alabama and one of the most prominent black Americans of his time, and expressed interest in helping higher education institutions. Washington urged him to help elementary grades as well by underwriting a program he envisioned for building new schools.

Julius Rosenwald

The first Rosenwald school opened in 1913, and the Rosenwald Fund was established four years later with the vast majority of its funds going toward school construction.

The Rosenwald grants had to be matched by local communities, and the schools were designed by Tuskegee architecture students.

Over 20 years, the program contributed some $4.3 million in seed money to build 5,357 public schools, shops, and teachers' residences in 15 states, from Texas to Maryland. By 1920, the program had grown so large that Rosenwald set up an office in Nashville, Tenn., to manage the enterprise.

Booker T. Washington

Rosenwald and Washington hoped their efforts would foster more collaboration and better relationships between African-Americans and local white leaders. That dream, by most accounts, was unrealized, and most of the schools' operating costs were woefully underfunded by the white school boards that oversaw them.

Washington himself was controversial. Some African-Americans rejected his view that vocational education and economic self-improvement should take priority over demands for social and political equality for blacks.

The Rosenwald school-building program operated until 1932, the year of the philanthropist's death.

The Rosenwald Fund continued until 1948, but shifted priorities to other projects to attempt to further black education and equality.

—JOETTA L. SACK

she produced telling results. Of 19 schools on the list, five were intact, two were altered beyond recognition, and one was in ruins. Evidence suggested that 10 had been destroyed. The intern was unable to find any evidence of one of the schools on the list, but found seven schools that appeared to be Rosenwald-like structures.

School historians recently discovered a long-abandoned school in Inez, N.C., a tiny community in rural Warren County. The faded structure is barely visible from the road, tucked in a field behind a row of chicken coops. Its door hangs open, revealing a jumble of desks.

While the Rosenwald schools in rural areas are more likely to still exist, many are decaying. Those in urban areas are most likely to have been destroyed as part of redevelopment. There are no estimates of the number of them still standing.

Some examples point to creative reuse of the buildings. In Asheboro, N.C., one seven-room school has been converted to apartments for the elderly. Others have been taken over by churches as classroom space, and some have become homes. Just a few, including a middle school in Winston-Salem, N.C., are still in use as schools.

Near Raleigh, St. Matthew Missionary Baptist Church renovated the St. Matthew School. Some church members once wanted to let the local fire department burn the wooden building—then severely dilapidated and surrounded by new development—as a training exercise, says Pryce Baldwin Jr., a member of the congregation. Today, it's used for meetings and youth programs.

Baldwin says he has worked to educate the church members and others—some of whom had unknowingly attended Rosenwald schools—about the history of the St. Matthew School.

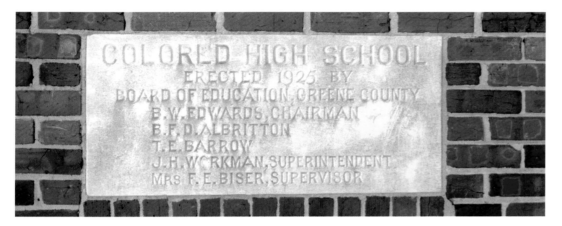

GREENE COUNTY TRAINING CENTER Snow Hill, N.C.

Snow Hill Colored High School was built in 1925. It later became the Greene County Training Center, which was a vocation-focused school for African-Americans. The building now houses a manufacturing business and serves as the administrative office for the group of local residents and alumni that is trying to restore the site as a community center.

"The more I travel the state, the more I look for them," he says. "We're losing a part of history."

NOT ALL OF THE ROSENWALD SCHOOLS SHUT DOWN when North Carolina communities began bowing to the integration demands stemming from the 1954 *Brown* decision; most remained segregated until the mid-1960s. The DuBois school stayed open until 1989 and was used as part of an eight-building high school campus that grew from the original site. It was one of the few Rosenwald schools that became integrated.

Usually, school boards closed those schools because they had not been well-maintained, and because whites objected to sending their children to schools in traditionally black neighborhoods.

Today, with six of the eight buildings boarded up, the campus has a hollow, abandoned feel. The two remaining buildings are used as a gym and a community center.

But the DuBois Rosenwald school has a legion of alumni working to restore it. So far, they have raised enough money to hire an architect and stabilize the structure. About 200 alumni, who still meet each year for a reunion, are working to raise the estimated $1.2 million needed to fully restore the school.

One alumna, Bettie Edwards Murchison, wants at least part of the building to become a museum that will "highlight the struggle African-American children had to get an education."

Murchison, who was one of the first black students that teachers sent to newly integrated white schools in the 1960s, has vivid memories of the graduation ceremonies, May Day events, and proms that made the DuBois school the hub of the community. When a student graduated from high school or even 8th grade, she remembers, it was such a source of pride that family members would come from all over the state for events that lasted a week.

"Graduation was a family and community accomplishment, not just the child's," she says.

Murchison works next door to the building, as the executive director of the DuBois Center, which provides social services and after-school programs to families. The center wants to create a vocational school and culinary arts school for local students, which could be incorporated into the Rosenwald structure, she said.

"We're trying to be creative, as much as we have to do," she says.

THE ERA OF INTEGRATION UNSHERED in by the *Brown* decision brought a downside as well as benefits for teachers and students who had attended Snow Hill Colored High School in Snow Hill, N.C., some alumni say. When they were given access to a better education system and sent to different schools, some say their community's cohesiveness and determination were damaged.

"When the schools integrated, we gained a lot, but we lost a lot," says JoAnn Stevens, who attended the school in the 1960s and later attended integrated schools. "When we began to get our freedom and rights, we lost some of our unity."

The school, now known as the Rosenwald Center, opened in 1925.

DUBOIS SCHOOL Wake Forest, N.C.
This Rosenwald school, like many others, is on the opposite side of the railroad tracks from local white neighborhoods. The decaying building has been empty since closing as a high school in 1989.

It later became the Greene County Training Center, a common designation for secondary schools that served African-Americans.

Stevens and others remember the site as a place not only for education, but also for love and lessons in life. It was one of the larger Rosenwald schools, with eight classrooms and a large auditorium.

"To a kid who'd never seen too much, it looked like a mansion to me," says Robert Briggs, who began school there as a kindergartner in 1928. He remembers students who arrived in horse-drawn buggies, and others who lived in the countryside and stayed with relatives in town on weeknights in order to receive an education. Parents grew crops of cotton and vegetables to sell to subsidize the school's programs, he said.

"The teachers had time for children, and love for the children," adds Stevens. "They treated you like part of their family, and you were going to learn."

But many students and teachers also understood that prejudice existed outside those walls.

Gwenoese Smith remembers that her father, the principal, had a fight every time he asked for basic supplies or services from the local school board. "Their thinking was, '*Why* do you need it?'" she says. "Everything had to be justified."

The school still has a legion of alumni and former teachers in the area, and alumni chapters in Washington, New York, and New Jersey, who want to restore the building as a cultural center.

The dark, red-brick building now appears vacant, with boarded front windows and a dusty driveway. But the narrow vestibule opens into an unexpectedly expansive room filled with colorful reams of fabric. Several African-American women sit at sewing machines fashioning pillows, bed linens, and other textile products. If

it weren't for this local business that rents the space for use as a factory, the former school likely would have been torn down years ago.

So far, the alumni group has raised about $40,000 of the estimated $750,000 needed to restore the school. The main goal, Stevens says, is to raise awareness about the school and its history.

"When I first started talking about Rosenwald, people didn't know what it was," she says. "Even after she explained the history, some people "didn't grasp the idea that the school was significant."

OTHER ROSENWALD SCHOOLS do not have such dedicated alumni groups. Some of those schools, though, have determined preservationists looking for buyers with deep pockets and an interest in restoring a significant part of the history of education for blacks.

Barbara Wishy has taken on the task of selling the Princeton Graded School, a blighted six-room, brick Rosenwald structure. Wishy, the director of the Endangered Properties Program at Preservation North Carolina, a nonprofit group, says that once a structure is designated "historic," her group can work with owners to place restrictions on the property's deed to prevent it from being torn down or severely altered after it is sold.

Located on the outskirts of Princeton, a town east of Raleigh, the Princeton Graded School was left to languish after schools were integrated following the *Brown* decision. A wing of the school was recently used as a day-care center, but the building now sits vacant.

A 1950s addition has been partially demolished, and old furniture, bikes, and boxes have been dumped across the property. Panes of

ST. MATTHEW SCHOOL Raleigh, N.C. Rosenwald schools were designed with rows of large windows to maximize natural lighting. Today, the old school at St. Matthew Missionary Baptist Church houses the church's youth ministries.

glass have been broken, and inside, old clothing and household objects litter the floors.

The school is owned by Elaine Mabson, who now lives in Maryland. In her application to have the school designated as historic, she says she recalls the buses that would leave before dawn to pick up black children around the countryside, and pass by the large, well-kept school for whites in the center of the town. Her mother, who died in 1999 and left Mabson the building, often told her stories about a man named Mr. Rosenwald who wanted to help them obtain an education.

In 1973, when the building was auctioned, Mabson's mother was living in Washington and hired a white man to go to North Carolina and bid on the property so it would not be torn down. When some of the local white leaders found out she bought the school, they rezoned the property as "residential," making it difficult to reuse, she said.

"Although they have removed the 'colored' and 'white' signs to designate territories, people in that town still know where their place is," Mabson wrote in the application. "I do not want anyone to forget how blacks were treated and why that building should stand. It represents the struggle that took place in Princeton in the early 1920s when blacks had the desire to learn, but were denied that right."

The town has since pressured her to tear down the structure, Mabson says. She says she is unable to afford the upkeep, and the zoning restriction makes it hard to run a profitable business there.

"I felt obligated to hold on to it because it meant so much to my mother," she says. "But even the community doesn't show that much interest as far as looking out for the building."

Preservation North Carolina is marketing the 5,000-square-foot building for $157,500. Wishy is optimistic that, eventually, someone will buy and restore it.

"We want to make sure it's not only sold, but protected," Wishy says. "We're not expecting it to be a quick turnover, but it will happen." ∎

Allison Shelley

Members of the junior varsity boys' soccer team practice at Wakefield High School in Arlington, Va.
Many members of the team are Hispanic or from families that recently immigrated from Africa.

In U.S. Schools, Race Still Counts

Despite Progress, Challenges Loom

BY CAROLINE HENDRIE

Many observers of the U.S. Supreme Court were expecting May 17, 1954, to be a run-of-the-mill Monday—until Chief Justice Earl Warren made a surprise announcement: He was ready to deliver the court's opinion in *Brown* v. *Board of Education of Topeka.*

"We conclude—unanimously—that in the field of public education the doctrine of 'separate but equal' has no place," he told those assembled that afternoon in the marble-and-mahogany courtroom. "Separate educational facilities are inherently unequal."

Since that historic moment half a century ago, much has changed in American life and education. By today's standards, the notion that black children could be consigned to separate schools solely because of their skin color—in a nation founded on principles of freedom and equality—seems unconscionable. Indeed, the nation's highest-ranking school official, U.S. Secretary of Education Rod Paige, is African-American.

Still, how many people would argue that race is irrelevant in contemporary American education? How many would say that the promise of "Equal Justice for All"—the words incised on the Supreme Court building's facade—has truly become a reality in the nation's public schools?

In the past five years, as test-based accounta-bility has come to dominate the public education agenda, the racial and ethnic "achievement gap" has risen to the top of policymakers' concerns. Eliminating disparities between blacks and Hispanics, on the one hand, and whites and Asian-Americans on the other, is a primary goal of the No Child Left Behind Act, the 2-year-old federal law that now exerts a powerful influence in elementary and secondary education.

Fifty years after racially segregated schooling was pronounced unconstitutional, one-race public schools, and even virtually one-race districts, still exist. Despite a growing number of thoroughly integrated schools, many remain overwhelmingly white or minority. And schools with many black and Hispanic children, especially if most of those pupils live in poverty, often come up short on standard measures of educational health.

Thus, for many of those steeped in the work of making policy and running schools, questions of race and education still matter—just as they did on the day Chief Justice Warren delivered the court's momentous ruling.

"Issues of race continue to be overpowering forces in American education," said Michael D. Casserly, the executive director of the Washington-based Council of the Great City Schools, "and the pre-eminent challenge for America in the century ahead."

In light of that challenge, *Education Week* is setting out to take stock of the role that race continues to play in American schools. This edition features the first installment of a five-part series, which will run in the months leading up to the *Brown* decision's 50th anniversary. *(See "About This Series," Page 30.)*

'Ultimate Hypocrisy'

The ruling commonly called *Brown* v. *Board of Education* actually decided four, consolidated cases, all challenging the practice of providing separate public schools for blacks and whites. Such segregation had long been shielded by the Supreme Court's 1896 ruling in *Plessy* v. *Ferguson*, which upheld "separate but equal" facilities for blacks and whites.

Besides the case out of Topeka, Kan., the others involved districts in Delaware, South Carolina, and Virginia. Because of distinctive legal issues, a fifth case, challenging segregated schools in the District of Columbia, was decided separately in *Bolling* v. *Sharpe*, a judgment announced the same day as the *Brown* ruling.

A year later, in a ruling known as *Brown II*, the Supreme Court vested local school authorities with chief responsibility for dismantling segregation, which at the time was nearly universal in the South and the states bordering it. That brief decision on May 31, 1955, famously ordered that the transition to nondiscriminatory schooling

These charts show the performance of African-American and non-Hispanic white students on the 2003 administration of the National Assessment of Educational Progress in 4th grade reading and 8th grade mathematics. This achievement gap has risen to the top of policymakers' concerns and is a major focus of the No Child Left Behind Act.

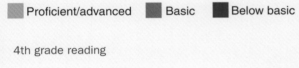

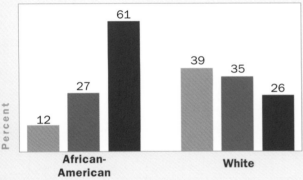

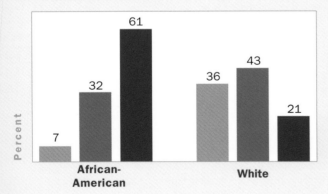

SOURCE: The Education Trust, 2003

proceed under the oversight of lower courts with "all deliberate speed."

As the 50th anniversary of the first *Brown* ruling approaches, the occasion has prompted an outpouring of conferences, books, articles, speeches, and studies that acknowledge the decision as a milestone in the nation's long march toward recovery from slavery.

Among some leaders engaged in those commemorations, a common lament is that Topic A in the *Brown* cases—the racial composition of public schools—has been shunted to the margins of public preoccupations.

"It's the ultimate hypocrisy if we go into 2004 celebrating *Brown* v. *Board of Education*, and all that has been accomplished, and we have nothing to say about the massive patterns of racial segregation in public education and in residential patterns that continue to be a hallmark of American life," said Theodore M. Shaw, the associate director-counsel of the NAACP Legal Defense and Educational Fund, the New York City-based organization that led the assault on Jim Crow education.

"*Brown* was about many things, but at the core of *Brown* was the notion that the government ought not be able to segregate people on the basis of race and then deprive them of equal opportunity," added Mr. Shaw, a member of the U.S. Department of Education's *Brown* anniversary commission.

Another commission member, Washington lawyer Judith A. Winston, said she also would love to see more communities in which white and minority parents banded together to fight for more integrated schools. But she is not terribly optimistic.

"What is at the heart of my concern ... is my belief that we have not gotten past the deeply ingrained racial stereotypes that have developed in this country over many decades," said Ms. Winston, who served as the Education Department's general counsel in the Clinton administration. "The fact of the matter is—and there's no nice way to put this—white families have been running away from the desegregation remedy in all parts of the country."

Despite defiance of desegregation that sometimes turned violent, school integration did increase steadily in the decades after *Brown* and continued through the 1980s.

Obstacles mounted, however, as court orders often proved insufficient to overcome housing patterns and steep declines in white enrollment in the urban districts where minority youngsters continue to be concentrated.

Questions of Access

So even though desegregation advocates often won in court, many plans to desegregate met with limited success. In the past decade, many have been scrapped, spurred by Supreme Court decisions that have stressed the temporary nature of court orders, the importance of local control of schools, and the limits on judicial authority to perpetuate desegregation plans.

"What makes it particularly difficult is that the opportunities for real desegregation in a great many inner cities are very limited," noted William L. Taylor, a Washington lawyer who is the chairman of the Citizens' Commission on Civil Rights, a private watchdog group that monitors the Education Department's enforcement of civil rights laws.

Today, most of the desegregation fights of the past half-century have been put to rest, and with them, much of the public attention to the issue.

And some say that is as it should be. Given the logistical and legal limits to promoting greater racial and ethnic balance in the schools, some analysts say it is appropriate that the debate has shifted to improving achievement among minority youngsters regardless of the demographic makeup of their classrooms.

After all, those observers say, ending the physical separation of the races was always seen by those battling segregation as a means to an end.

"The real issue was whether everybody was going to have access to educational quality of equal worth," said Mr. Casserly, whose group represents large-city school systems. "The issue has evolved so that in some ways it has returned to its roots."

For Secretary Paige, himself a graduate of segregated schools in his native Mississippi, the No Child Left Behind Act is "the logical next step" to the long and far-flung court battles over desegregation that followed *Brown*. In a Jan. 7 speech in Washington in which he reflected on the *Brown* decision's legacy, Mr. Paige praised the law's insistence that schools report on the performance of students in various racial and ethnic groups and bring them up to academic snuff.

"Equality of opportunity must be more than just a statement of law; it must be a matter of fact," Mr. Paige said. "And factually speaking, this country does not yet promote equal opportunities for millions of children. That is why the No Child Left Behind Act is so important. After 50 years, we still have a lot of work to do."

Mr. Paige added in an interview that the *Brown* case aimed to give black children access to schools from which they had been excluded, but that "we know now because of the 50 years of experience we've had that something else is necessary."

"The issue of access to quality education and access to achievement is now the place we need to get to."

Rossi Ray-Taylor, Executive Director
Minority Student Achievement Network

John Zich

That "something else" still involves access, but in a way that is different from in the past, said Rossi Ray-Taylor, a former district superintendent in Michigan who is now the executive director of the Minority Student Achievement Network.

"Fifty years ago, schools attended by African-Americans were hugely underresourced, so it was really an issue of access to resources," said Ms. Ray-Taylor, whose network includes 21 generally well-off school systems concerned about closing racial gaps in achievement. "The issue of

access to quality education and access to achievement is now the place we need to get to. How are we going to teach every kid so they are going to get access to outcomes?"

'Frightening' Gaps

Perhaps the best-known statistics about the inequality of those outcomes come from the National Assessment of Educational Progress, the government-run testing program known as "the nation's report card."

Versions of NAEP designed to provide trend data were last given in 1999, and in that year, reading and math tests of 17-year-olds showed that African-American and Hispanic youngsters that age were, on average, scoring at levels roughly on a par with 13-year-old whites.

As the scholars Abigail Thernstrom and Stephan Thernstrom note in their 2003 book *No Excuses: Closing the Racial Gap in Learning*, black youngsters nearing the end of high school, on average, posted slightly lower scores than white 8th graders in both reading and U.S. history, and much lower scores in mathematics and geography. Average scores among Hispanics were slightly better than those for blacks.

Arguing that this "frightening," four-year skills gap has become a major policy priority only in the past five years, Ms. Thernstrom said in a recent interview that valuable time has been lost in addressing it. Ms. Thernstrom, a member of the Massachusetts state board of education, and her husband, a professor at Harvard University, are both senior fellows at the Manhattan Institute, a think tank in New York City.

"The gap itself has been a hush-hush topic until very recently," she said. "This discussion should have started a long time ago."

Definition of Regions

SOUTH:
Ala., Ark., Fla., Ga., La., Miss., N.C., S.C., Tenn., Texas, and Va.

"BORDER":
Del., Ky., Md., Mo., Okla., and W.Va.

NORTHEAST:
Conn., Maine, Mass., N.H., N.J., N.Y., Pa., R.I., and Vt.

MIDWEST:
Ill., Ind., Iowa, Kan., Mich., Minn., Neb., N.D., Ohio, S.D., and Wis.

WEST:
Ariz., Calif., Colo., Mont., Nev., N.M., Ore., Utah, Wash., and Wyo.

Note: Alaska and Hawaii are excluded from most parts of this study because of their unique ethnic compositions and isolation from the regions studied here.

SOURCE: *"Brown* at 50: King's Dream or *Plessy's* Nightmare?,"
Gary Orfield and Chungmei Lee, 2004.

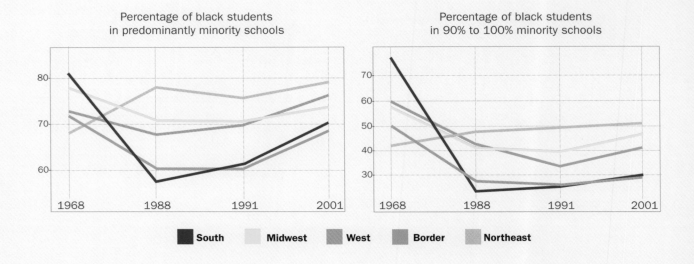

Percentage of black students in predominantly minority schools

Percentage of black students in 90% to 100% minority schools

■ South   ■ Midwest   ■ West   ■ Border   ■ Northeast

To many analysts, the skills gap is all the more troubling because during the 1990s, black and Hispanic students gave back a good bit of the progress they had made in catching up in the previous two decades.

"There was a tremendous amount of gap-narrowing in the '70s and '80s, and somewhere around 1990, that gap-narrowing stopped," observed Craig D. Jerald, a senior policy analyst at the Education Trust, a Washington-based organization that advocates improvement in the education of poor and minority students. "By and large, the gaps have stayed the same since."

The causes of the nation's racial fault lines in educational attainment remain poorly understood.

"Most big social facts have more than one explanation, and this is no exception," said Christopher Jencks, a professor of social policy at Harvard's John F. Kennedy School of Government and a co-editor of the 1998 book *The Black-White Test Score Gap*.

An Unwanted Guest

Among the perennial questions has been the respective roles played by schools and family. For example, the landmark 1966 report *Equality of Educational Opportunity* by the sociologist James S. Coleman sparked controversy in part because it underscored the importance of family background in influencing achievement.

In their 1998 book, Mr. Jencks and co-editor Meredith Phillips of the University of California, Los Angeles, concluded that much more research was needed on both in-school and outside influences, including parental behavior, to figure out how best to bridge the gap.

"Although we believe that improving the nation's schools could reduce the black-white test-score gap, we do not believe that schools alone can eliminate it," they wrote.

Seconding that view is an Educational Testing Service researcher, Paul E. Barton, who published a study last year identifying 14 in-school and out-of-school factors linked to student achievement—ranging from rigorous coursework and teacher preparation to children's birth weight and television viewing—in which blacks and Hispanics suffered disadvantages compared with whites.

"Gaps in school achievement ... have deep roots—deep in out-of-school experiences and deep in the structures of schools," Mr. Barton concludes in "Parsing the Achievement Gap" from the Princeton, N.J.-based ETS. "Inequality is like an unwanted guest who comes early and stays late."

Despite the complex origins of the achievement disparities, recent NAEP scores show some evidence that the tide may be turning. For example, black 4th graders narrowed their gap with whites in both reading and math between 1992 and 2003 on the version of NAEP designed to measure current performance across the nation and in the states.

Moreover, examples are multiplying of individual schools, districts, and even states that have made solid, and even startling, advances in closing skills gaps.

Few see grounds for celebrating, though, at a time when the link between what students learn and their future prospects has never been stronger.

"There's no grounds for complacency," Ms. Thernstrom said.

To some longtime desegregation researchers, the achievement gap is prime evidence for why the nation should not turn its back on the goal of integrated schooling.

Among them is Gary Orfield, a Harvard University professor and a co-director of its Civil Rights Project. Starting with a 1994 book he co-wrote called *Dismantling Desegregation*, Mr. Orfield and others affiliated with the project have produced a steady stream of reports decrying the "resegregation" of American schools—a trend they link to the widening of the achievement gap.

Legal Barriers

Mr. Orfield points a finger squarely at the Supreme Court for erecting formidable legal

Black Students' Exposure to Whites Found Waning

Black students' exposure to white classmates has dwindled in many districts that have been released from court orders to desegregate over the past decade, Harvard University researchers say in a new report.

Timed to coincide with the Jan. 19 holiday honoring the Rev. Martin Luther King Jr., the report says that the continued prevalence of schools with high concentrations of minority students from poor families shows that the civil rights giant's hopes for a color-blind society have yet to be fulfilled.

"When we celebrate Martin Luther King Day, children in our schools often recite the 'I Have a Dream' speech as if it were a reality," says a draft version of the report by the Harvard Civil Rights Project. "Students are rarely told that Dr. King also had a nightmare, ... King saw the ghetto and its schools as a nightmare for black society."

Brown Districts Profiled

Co-written by Civil Rights Project co-director Gary Orfield and researcher Chungmei Lee, the report offers trend data on school integration at the national, regional, and state levels.

The report also points out that the districts involved in the cases that resulted in the *Brown* v. *Board of Education of Topeka* ruling in 1954— a watershed decision nearing its golden anniversary—vary widely in the racial composition of their schools.

"The legacy we are celebrating is mixed and the future is uncertain," the report says.

In light of the trend toward ending long-standing desegregation orders, the report examines changes in schools' racial composition in 35 districts freed from court supervision since an important U.S. Supreme Court ruling in 1991.

The high court justices approved Oklahoma City's return to neighborhood schools in that ruling, and made clear that lower courts should release from oversight districts that had complied in good faith and remedied past discrimination as much as is practical.

In the districts studied, the researchers calculated the change in the percentage of white students in the school of the average black student from 1991 to 2002. They found that only four saw gains in that measure of interracial exposure. Twenty-two of the districts saw drops of 10 percent or greater.

Some researchers have questioned Mr. Orfield's portrayal of drops in black students' exposure to white students as evidence of resegregation.

The report acknowledges that the situations in the 35 districts varied. Some had kept their desegregation plans despite the end of court supervision; others scrapped those plans even before a judge had declared them unitary.

Overall, the report stresses that much has changed since 1954, when 17 states and the District of Columbia had state-sanctioned school segregation.

Yet it also cautions that the gains may be slipping away. "We are celebrating a vic-tory over segregation that is being abandoned," the report says.

—CAROLINE HENDRIE

"Brown at 50: King's Dream or the *Plessy* Nightmare?"
is available at www.civilrightsproject.harvard.edu.

barriers to cross-district desegregation plans, especially in a major 1974 ruling involving Detroit and its suburbs known as *Milliken* v. *Bradley*. He also faults the high court for other decisions that prompted federal judges to close the books on many desegregation cases in recent years.

"In many districts where court-ordered desegregation was ended in the past decade, there has been a major increase in segregation," says a report co-written by Mr. Orfield that is slated for release this week. "The courts assumed that the forces that produced segregation and inequality had been cured. They have not." *(See story, this page.)*

Titled "*Brown* at 50: King's Dream or the *Plessy* Nightmare," the new report points out that amid continuing demographic changes, the public schools have become nearly 40 percent nonwhite. Key factors cited include a surge in immigration of Hispanics, as well as an influx of Asian-Americans.

"In these circumstances, a civil rights policy based on a black-white paradigm about white exclusion of blacks does not make much sense," the report says.

Still, a decline in African-American students' exposure to non-Hispanic white students in public schools is a recurrent concern of the Civil Rights Project.

More than 36 percent of black students went to public schools that were majority white in 1988, but that proportion fell to 30 percent over the next dozen years, according to the report. The trend was more pronounced in the South. From 1954, when almost no African-Americans attended majority-white schools, the proportion steadily climbed to a high-water mark of 43.5 percent in 1988, when the trend started to reverse, the report says. By 2001,

"If we really do want to reach a point where we no longer have to employ affirmative action, then we as a nation have to roll up our sleeves."

Theodore M. Shaw, Associate Director-Counsel
NAACP Legal Defense and Education Fund

the figure had slid to 30 percent.

Latino youngsters' exposure to non-Hispanic white schoolmates was also on the decline as of 2001, with the typical Latino student attending public schools with white populations of 28 percent. By contrast, Asian and Native American students on average attended schools in which 45 percent of students were non-Hispanic whites.

White students, meanwhile, were attending public schools that were on average 79 percent white.

Some scholars take issue with the Civil Rights Project's emphasis on minority exposure to whites, arguing that lessened exposure is to be expected in part because the percentage of whites in the student population is steadily declining.

But Mr. Orfield says that demographics alone fail to explain why blacks' exposure to white students climbed during the period of court-ordered desegregation—especially in the South—and then waned as those orders wound down.

"Public schools were becoming less white ever since *Brown*, and we got this pattern of increasing desegregation up until the late 1980s," he said. "And then consistently it turns in the opposite direction."

Carrying On

One ray of hope for proponents of integration came early last summer when the Supreme Court handed down a 5-4 decision in *Grutter* v. *Bollinger*, a closely watched case involving admissions practices at the University of Michigan law school.

With a nod toward the *Brown* decision, the one-justice majority held that promoting racial and ethnic diversity in the classroom could, under some circumstances, justify carefully crafted affirmative action policies.

Legal analysts from differing perspectives agree that the decision might help K-12 districts defend race-conscious practices aimed at fostering diverse student enrollments in selective academic programs. But for other areas in which schools might want to consider race and ethnicity—in general student-assignment policies, say, or transfer decisions—the ruling's applicability to the elementary and secondary levels is less clear.

"Before Michigan, I would have said that the courts had pretty much struck down race-based policies," said Alfred A. Lindseth, an Atlanta lawyer who has helped districts and states win release from desegregation court orders. "Michigan has changed the situation. It's muddied the waters."

Mr. Taylor of the Citizens' Commission on Civil Rights, whose work has been mainly in securing desegregation orders, not ending them, said he believed the Michigan case gave strong ammunition to districts wishing to pursue voluntary desegregation programs, such as racially balanced magnet schools. Beyond that, he said, "I think we still have to sort it out."

Toward the end of Justice Sandra Day O'Connor's majority opinion in *Grutter*, she noted that the number of black and Hispanic applicants to the law school with high grades and test scores had risen over the previous generation. Given that progress, she wrote, the court "expects that 25 years from now, the use of racial preferences will no longer be necessary" to ensure that university classrooms are racially and ethnically diverse.

How that 25-year timetable will be interpreted in the future—as a deadline, or as merely a hope—remains unclear. But two generations after the *Brown* decision, those carrying the torch of desegregated schooling say they have no plans to rest on their laurels.

"If we really do want to reach a point where we no longer have to employ affirmative action," Mr. Shaw said, "then we as a nation need to roll up our sleeves and rededicate ourselves to the work that we started so long ago." ∎

Members and staff of the federal *Brown* anniversary commission tour the new museum in Topeka, Kan. It tells the story of the case and the related battles for civil rights and desegregation that it helped fuel.

Thad Allton

Historic Topeka School Hosts Museum Dedicated to *Brown*

A 'Powerful Reminder' of Civil Rights Struggle

BY MARK WALSH
Topeka, Kan.

The Monroe School building bore a large "For Auction" sign in 1990, when a staff member of the Brown Foundation for Educational Excellence drove by one day.

For decades, Monroe was one of four segregated grade schools where the Topeka board of education assigned black schoolchildren. The building had been through many permutations since it closed in 1975: a warehouse, a church meeting place, a clothing-distribution center. It had even housed a dentist's office. Its long-term future was a question mark.

But the Brown Foundation would soon embark on a mission to preserve a local and national historic site. And next month, years of effort to restore the Monroe School will culminate in its dedication as a museum depicting the story of the *Brown* v. *Board of Education of Topeka* case and related battles for desegregation and civil rights.

"The story of the *Brown* case is complex, but it is very compelling," said Stephen E. Adams, the

Thad Allton

Members of the federal commission marking the 50th anniversary of the *Brown* decision view the former kindergarten room of the segregated Monroe School attended by Linda Brown, whose father, Oliver, joined in filing the lawsuit.

"This is a site where we want people to do a lot of thinking."

Stephen E. Adams
Superintendent, *Brown* v. *Board of Education* National Historic Site

National Park Service's superintendent of the national historic site at the Monroe School, who led a preview tour of the museum last month.

"We want people to understand the significance and the history of the case," he said. "This is a site where we want people to do a lot of thinking."

Monroe School was where Linda Brown, the daughter of local railroad worker and minister Oliver L. Brown, was enrolled when Mr. Brown in 1950 unsuccessfully sought to enroll her in a whites-only school closer to their home. The Browns would become one of 13 families to challenge segregated schools in Topeka in a lawsuit organized by the National Association for the Advancement of Colored People.

The rest, of course, is history. Fifty years ago next month, the U.S. Supreme Court declared segregation of the races in public education unconstitutional. It was no accident that the court placed the Kansas case at the top of its opinions covering consolidated school segregation cases that also came from Delaware, the District of Columbia, South Carolina, and Virginia. The justices reached out to include the heartland of the nation in a decision that they knew would bring wrenching changes, especially in the South.

'White' or 'Colored'

The renovated Monroe School will be dedicated on May 17, exactly 50 years after the *Brown* ruling. U.S. Secretary of Education Rod Paige is scheduled to attend, and organizers have received hints from the White House that President Bush may be there, too.

The day will cap a yearlong commemoration of the historic case that has included scholarly conferences, museum exhibits, children's writing contests, and other events. *(See box, Page 17.)*

But the anniversary also will likely usher in fresh interest in the case and the history of the U.S. civil rights movement. Organizers hope that young people's curiosity to learn more about the story of the case will be piqued.

Daniel Holt, a member of the federal *Brown* v. *Board of Education* 50th Anniversary Commission and the director of the Dwight D. Eisenhower Presidential Library, said that if experience is any guide, "you're going to get a lot more attention after May 17 than you have before."

Last month, the commission—which includes appointees from each of the jurisdictions involved in the consolidated Supreme Court cases—got a preview of the Brown museum. *Education Week* was allowed to go along as museum staff members showed off the restored Monroe School and its exhibits, which were substantially complete but awaiting some final touches.

When it opens to the public, visitors entering the building will immediately be given a choice of passing through entryways marked "white" or "colored." In the school's auditorium, state-of-the-art video displays tell the story of how segregated schools came to be.

Next, in the "Education and Justice" exhibit room, visitors have to pass through a gantlet of

Linda Brown, in foreground, attends class at the segregated Monroe School in 1953.

Commemorating the *Brown* Decision

Here is a sampling of events marking the 50th anniversary of *Brown* v. *Board of Education of Topeka*, the May 17, 1954, U.S. Supreme Court decision overturning racial segregation in public schools.

April 17 *Simple Justice: The History of Brown v. Board of Education and Black America's Struggle for Equality* is republished in an expanded, revised edition. Author Richard Kluger traces the origins of the lawsuits that were later considered together by the U.S. Supreme Court and analyzes the country's progress on racial issues since the book's first publication in 1975. Publisher's Web site: www.randomhouse.com/knopf.

April 23 *Black, White and Brown: The School Desegregation Case in Retrospect* is published by the Supreme Court Historical Society and Congressional Quarterly Press, with a preface by Chief Justice William H. Rehnquist. In this collection of essays, scholars examine the cases that eroded the "separate but equal" doctrine laid down by the high court in 1896, the challenge of enforcing *Brown*, and changes over time in views of *Brown*. Publisher's Web site: www.cqpress.com.

April 29 The American Bar Association's Brown Commission hosts a panel discussion at the National Constitution Center in Philadelphia, moderated by Harvard University law professor Charles Ogletree, exploring the legal, ethical, and public-policy issues emanating from the decision. ABA Web site: www.abanet.org.

May 11 The Cato Institute in Washington sponsors a book forum entitled "Educational Freedom in Urban America: *Brown* v. *Board* After Half a Century." Participants include Rod Paige, U.S. secretary of education; Gerard Robinson, University of Virginia; Casey Lartigue, Fight for Children; Clint Bolick, School Choice Alliance; and Howard Fuller, Institute for the Transformation of Learning, Marquette University. Cato Web site: www.cato.org.

May 14-17 The National Association for the Advancement of Colored People, whose litigators argued the *Brown* case before the Supreme Court, holds several events to commemorate the anniversary. A three-day "Summit of the States" will be held May 14-16 in Topeka, Kan., where participants will discuss states' plans to reach educational equity. On May 17, NAACP officials will join Kansas Gov. Kathleen Sebelius and leaders of the Brown Foundation in a commemorative rally on the steps of the state Capitol in Topeka. Also on May 17, the NAACP, the NAACP Legal Defense and Educational Fund, and Howard University will host an awards gala in Washington honoring people and groups that played significant roles in the Brown decision. NAACP Web site: www.naacp.org.

May 15 New York and New Jersey high school students who have been participating in a two-year research project on race and persistent inequality in schools will perform "Echoes of *Brown*: 50 Years Later." The New York City invitation-only performance combines dance and poetry with the students' videotaped discussions with civil rights pioneers. Michelle Fine, a professor of psychology and urban education at the City University of New York's graduate center, has overseen the students' work to document the effects of the *Brown* decision. A DVD and book and a series of scholarly reports also will be released. Information: mfine@gc.cuny.edu.

May 15 The National Museum of American History, part of the Smithsonian Institution in Washington, opens a yearlong exhibit tracing the historical events that led up to and were influenced by the *Brown* decision. The exhibit centers on how the case transformed the country, including a look at segregated American life and the role education played in ending it; profiles of prominent figures in the *Brown* case; and an examination of how the legal arguments worked their way to the Supreme Court. Museum Web site: americanhistory.si.edu/.

May 17-19 New York University hosts a conference, "*Brown* Plus 50: A Renewed Agenda for Social Justice," in New York City. Kicking off the conference will be a "teach-in" for high school students from across the country, who can participate in person or via webcast. The conference will also include nationally webcast forums and discussion sessions on the legacies of *Brown*, the difficulty of putting the decision into practice, and policy direction for the future. NYU Web site: www.nyu.edu.

Ongoing "Courage, the Carolina Story That Changed America," an exhibit exploring the Southern roots of the *Brown* case, is on display until Aug. 15 at the Levine Museum of the New South in Charlotte, N.C. Museum Web site: www.museumofthenewsouth.org.

video screens showing historical footage of white opponents of desegregation, including some who spew racial epithets, providing a sense of what the desegregation pioneers faced. The museum also has a room devoted to the legacy and effects of the *Brown* case, both in the United States and around the world.

Finally, visitors end up in the school's former kindergarten room, where they can record their reactions to the exhibits.

The second floor houses a resource center for students and others, as well as the offices of the museum staff and the Brown Foundation, which was privately founded in 1988 to preserve the legacy of the case.

Roger Wilkins, a member of the *Brown* commission and a professor of American history and culture at George Mason University in Fairfax, Va., stopped as he toured the exhibit on March 17 to examine a famous photo of Elizabeth Eckford, one of the black students who desegregated Little Rock's Central High School in 1957. In the picture, Ms. Eckford is walking alone near the school, taunted by several whites.

"Her classmates said she never recovered from that," Mr. Wilkins observed.

The Little Rock photo demonstrates the approach the organizers of the Brown museum have taken. Instead of offering a detailed exhibit about the history of the Topeka case, the museum at the *Brown* v. *Board of Education* National Historic Site embraces the larger story of the struggle for civil rights.

"It's very well done," said Mr. Wilkins. "If you were born into segregation, as I was, it's a powerful reminder of childhood."

But the museum's broader approach didn't sit well with another member of the *Brown* commission. Joseph A. De Laine Jr., the son of the min-

Commission members gather outside the former Monroe School in Topeka, Kan., for a tour of the exhibits that opened in May 2004 to mark the anniversary of the historic U.S. Supreme Court decision.

ister who launched the South Carolina desegregation case, *Briggs* v. *Elliott*, told Mr. Adams during the tour that he was worried that students might come away from the museum without learning much about the other cases.

"I give them an A for effort," Mr. De Laine said outside the school. "But I think it somewhat overemphasizes the civil rights era of the '60s, and doesn't have enough on the *Brown* era of the 1950s."

In fact, one focus of the *Brown* commission, whose members were selected by President Bush, Secretary Paige, U.S. Chief Justice William H.

Rehnquist, and others, has been to shine a light on all five desegregation cases that the Supreme Court decided on that day in 1954. The commission has held its meetings over the past 18 months in sites connected to the four state cases that made up *Brown*, and the District of Columbia case, for which the Supreme Court issued the separate opinion known as *Bolling* v. *Sharpe*.

Mr. Adams told Mr. De Laine that when all the exhibits are in place, visitors will get a sense of the history of all five cases. "We never discussed that this was just going to be about Topeka," Mr. Adams said later. "It isn't just about one little girl."

One of the interactive exhibits teaches some of the "fact or fiction" of the *Brown* case. One statement offered is: "Oliver Brown single-handedly sued the Topeka School Board on behalf of his daughter." When visitors seek the answer, they learn: "No, Oliver Brown was among a group of 13 parents who brought a class action" challenging segregated schools.

The Only Man

According to most historical accounts—including *Simple Justice*, the widely praised 1975 book by Richard Kluger—Mr. Brown's name appeared first among the plaintiffs in the Topeka lawsuit because he was the only man among the parents. The suit challenged the Topeka system's policy of segregating white and black pupils in its 22 K-6 grade schools. Four were designated for black children and 18 for whites.

The segregation policy, which Kansas law permitted but did not require for the largest school systems in the state, did not apply to Topeka's junior and senior high schools, which were integrated in the classroom, although not necessarily in after-school activities.

In September 1950, Mr. Brown walked his eldest daughter, Linda, a few blocks from their home and tried to enroll her in the all-white Sumner School. They were turned down. Mr. Kluger writes that Mr. Brown and other black parents whose children faced long daily trips to the city's black schools were most likely approached by McKinley Burnett, the head of the NAACP branch in Topeka, to join the lawsuit.

At a conference at the University of Kansas, in Lawrence, last month, Mr. Burnett's daughter, Maurita Burnett Davis, recalled that her father was often asked why he didn't file suit on behalf of his own children.

"We lived next door to the Monroe School and did not have to pass another school to get there," she explained.

The lawsuit was tried in 1951 before a special three-judge U.S. District Court panel at the federal courthouse in Topeka. Thurgood Marshall, who directed the NAACP Legal Defense Fund's national strategy for attacking segregation in schools, did not come to Topeka, but defense-fund lawyers Robert L. Carter and Jack Greenberg joined local lawyers to attack the Topeka policy.

In the summer of 1951, the trial court ruled for the Topeka board of education. Judge Walter A. Huxman wrote that the "separate but equal" doctrine of the Supreme Court's 1896 *Plessy* v. *Ferguson* decision was still the law of the land. But the opinion ultimately played a significant role in the Supreme Court's decision in the *Brown* case. The Topeka court issued findings of fact that racial segregation "had a detrimental effect on the black schoolchildren."

The opinion was viewed by many legal observers as sympathetic to desegregation, with its findings forcing the Supreme Court to confront directly the separate-but-equal doctrine.

The Topeka school board dropped its segregation policy in 1953. Following the 1954 ruling by the high court, the desegregation case would become dormant for many years until it was revived in the late 1970s by black parents who argued that there were still vestiges of segregation in the school system here.

After more desegregation efforts and a lengthy series of court rulings, the Topeka district was declared "unitary," or free of the vestiges of a dual system, in 1999.

Today, the enrollment of the 14,000-student district is 49 percent white, 22 percent black, and 15 percent Hispanic. The rest of the students are either multiracial, Asian, or Native American.

'Hallelujah Time'

The Brown Foundation was fairly new when the staff member came across the auction sign in front of the school. But the foundation, led by Cheryl Brown Henderson, Oliver Brown's youngest daughter, sprang into action, trying to raise money to purchase the site.

With the backing of the Brown Foundation, the federal Trust for Public Land bought the school in 1991, and the next year Congress passed legislation establishing the *Brown* v. *Board of Education* National Historic Site. After that, the foundation and the National Park Service began a long planning process to restore the building and develop the museum.

The federal government has provided more than $11 million for the site, not all of which has been spent, said Mr. Adams of the National Park Service.

At the University of Kansas conference, held March 14-17, one of the participants was Leola Brown Montgomery, the widow of Oliver Brown, who died in 1961. She recalled how her first husband had been active in the local NAACP, which led to his involvement in the case.

When the Supreme Court ruled on May 17, 1954, it was approaching lunchtime in Topeka. Mrs. Montgomery, who is 83 and still lives in Topeka, recalled where she was when she heard the news. "I was home doing the family ironing," she said. "When that came down, I couldn't hardly wait for the family to get home."

When Mr. Brown arrived at their modest home on First Street, he said, " 'Thanks be to God,' " his wife recalled. "We had a hallelujah time." ■

Commission on *Brown* Anniversary Draws Mixed Reviews for Its Work

BY CATHERINE GEWERTZ

A year and a half ago, a federal commission began work to commemorate the 50th anniversary of the U.S. Supreme Court decision outlawing racial segregation in public schools. Now, as the May 17 date approaches, assessments of its accomplishments range from glowing to disappointing.

The *Brown* v. *Board of Education* 50th Anniversary Commission is drawing both praise and criticism from nationally prominent figures in education, civil rights, and government—including its own commissioners.

Some credit the panel with raising public awareness of the cases from Delaware, Kansas, South Carolina, and Virginia that were decided collectively in *Brown*, along with a companion case from the nation's capital, and with sparking dialogue about racial disparities that persist in public schools. Others complain that it has had little impact.

The assessments come as the commission prepares to take part in one of the higher-profile events designed to commemorate the ruling—the formal dedication on May 17 of a national historic site in Topeka, Kan. The site was once a segregated school for black students. *(See Education Week, April 7, 2004.)*

"They've done great work," said U.S. Sen. Sam Brownback, one of three Kansas Republicans who spearheaded the federal legislation that created the

Some members of the *Brown* commission gather in Topeka, Kan., at the museum that commemorates the landmark case. They include: back row, left to right, Lacy B. Ward Jr., Carolyn N. Sawyer, Stephen E. Adams, Dennis C. Hayes; middle row, Wan Kim, Littleton P. Mitchell, Eric Rosen, Roger Wilkins; front row, Roger L. Gregory, Josephine A. Robertson, Joseph A. De Laine Jr.

Thad Allton

panel. "You're seeing a lot more interest, and a lot more understanding of the *Brown* case."

'Not Very Visible'

But William L. Taylor, a nationally known civil rights lawyer who has worked on school desegregation cases, said he has heard little talk about the commission or its work. His comments echoed those of other prominent scholars, activists, and policymakers who said they knew little of the panel's activities.

"I would think that one of the functions is to have

a public presence to talk about the significance of *Brown*," Mr. Taylor said. "But it's not very visible."

Congress established a 22-member commission, according to the statute, to "encourage, plan, develop, and coordinate observances of" the anniversary of the *Brown* v. *Board of Education of Topeka* decision through "public education activities and initiatives" such as lectures, writing contests, and public-awareness campaigns. The panel was to work jointly with the U.S. Department of Education and the Brown Foundation for Educational Equity, Excellence, and Research, a nonprofit organization based in Topeka.

President Bush, in consultation with Congress, appointed half the members, drawing from the regions that produced the *Brown* cases. The rest were chosen by the Education Department, the U.S. Department of Justice, the chief justice of the United States, the Brown Foundation, the NAACP Legal Defense and Educational Fund, and the National Park Service, which oversees the Topeka historic site.

Since November 2002, when the panel began its work, it has held six public meetings in localities connected to the history of the *Brown* cases. At each site, panelists met with local leaders, toured historic areas, and hosted public discussions.

It has also hosted five forums around the country, some of which drew several hundred attendees. Topics included analyses of *Brown* from varying perspectives, such as its implications for the nation's growing Latino population, and the roles female activists and religious communities played in the case.

The panel also issued monthly e-mail newsletters announcing its own and other *Brown* commemorative events. In conjunction with National History Day, a University of Maryland-based project that runs a national historical-research competition each year, the panel sponsored an essay contest for students in grades 6-12 about the significance of *Brown* that drew more than 3,600 entries. Three winners are to be announced May 17.

Commissioner Cheryl Brown Henderson, who heads the Brown Foundation and whose father, Oliver L. Brown, was the lead plaintiff in the Topeka case, said she worked with the Kansas congressional delegation to pass the law creating the commission because she believed there should be a federal presence in the *Brown* anniversary.

Ms. Henderson said she was satisfied that goal was met and believes that the commission "was

able to get people thinking."

Brian W. Jones, the Education Department's general counsel and a co-chairman of the panel, said the commission did a great job making the public aware of the compelling personal stories that led to the litigation, and presenting the "larger issues" that arose from it.

'A Little Frustrated'

But some commissioners and observers are frustrated that the panel hasn't done more.

Joseph A. De Laine Jr., a commissioner whose father was a leader in the South Carolina school-desegregation movement, said he was glad the panel sparked some increased recognition of the cases. But he wishes it could have reached more people, especially in urban areas with racially diverse populations. "So I'm a little frustrated," he said.

The law authorized $250,000 for the panel, but only $200,000 was appropriated, and not until October 2003, nearly a year after the panel began its work. Its annual reports show that it used about $120,000 of Education Department funds and received more than $67,000 worth of services and supplies from business and education groups.

A small budget and a commemorative mission meant that the panel was "crippled from the start" in making an impact on the issues raised by *Brown*, said Christopher Edley Jr., a Harvard University law professor who advised President Clinton on affirmative action. To Mr. Edley, the panel's origins reflect a regrettable message from the Bush administration.

"The very least that any sitting president could have done for such a momentous historical event was to sponsor some commemorative exercise," he said. "But I think an inspired, deep commitment to

realizing the aspirations of *Brown* would have pointed to a much more ambitious effort."

Commissioner John H. Jackson, the national education director of the National Association for the Advancement of Colored People—which is hosting *Brown* events of its own—said he had hoped the commission would shape its public programs to provide more of a strategy to tackle racial disparities in schools. He learned only after being named to the panel how narrowly the law defined the group's mission, he said.

"When you develop a commission and constrain it where it doesn't have a substantive voice," he said, "it would raise questions as to whether or not the administration is just developing the commission to window-dress *Brown*'s 50th anniversary."

Many people argued that it wasn't the commission's role to have an impact on policy.

Tom Loveless, the director of the Brown Center on Education Policy at the Brookings Institution, a Washington think tank, said such commissions rarely draw wide public notice.

Ralph F. Boyd Jr., a former assistant U.S. attorney general for civil rights who co-chaired the commission before leaving his Justice Department job last year, backed the commission's work as "meaningful and substantive."

"People make [critical] comments because they have their own agenda, and if the commission doesn't do what their agenda is, they view it as nonsubstantive," he said.

Commissioner Deborah Dandridge, who is an archivist for the African-American collection at the University of Kansas libraries, said that "making policy or suggestions was not our focus.

"Our mission was simply to highlight the case and inform people of its historical significance," she said. "And I think it turned out to be a job well done." ∎

Students Less Upbeat Than Teachers on Race Relations

Integration Not Viewed as Key to Achievement

BY KARLA SCOON REID

An overwhelming majority of public school teachers and students believe that racially integrated schooling is important, a national poll commissioned by *Education Week* suggests.

But when asked what effect racially diverse environments have on achievement, half of teachers and three-quarters of students responded that integrated classes have no impact on student learning.

The survey, which gauges racial attitudes in schools a half-century after the U.S. Supreme Court struck down separate schooling for black and white students, found differences between teachers and students on questions of race and education.

Teachers depicted more positive cultural climates in their schools than did students, who were more likely to report that racial tensions exist and that teachers have lower expectations for black and Hispanic students.

The poll by Harris Interactive of Rochester, N.Y., was conducted online, using self-administered questionnaires, with a nationally representative sample of 2,591 public school teachers and 1,102 students in grades 7-12 in February and March.

Sixty-five percent of all teachers surveyed agreed that the goal of school integration in *Brown* v. *Board of Education of Topeka*, decided 50 years ago next week, has been met. And 60 percent of teachers said they believe that the United States offers equal academic opportunities for students of all races.

But there was a marked divide in responses from teachers of different racial and ethnic backgrounds.

Majorities of black (67 percent) and Hispanic (54 percent) teachers believed diverse classes would improve student learning, compared with 44 percent of white teachers.

While 69 percent of white teachers and 60 percent of Hispanic teachers said racially integrated schooling has been achieved, only 31 percent of black teachers agreed. When asked whether they thought equal academic opportunities were available to students regardless of race, 63 percent of white teachers and 52 percent of Hispanic teachers agreed, compared with just 28 percent of the black teachers polled.

A separate national online query of 3,698 U.S. adults by Harris Interactive this spring found similar attitudes. While 59 percent of the white respondents polled believed that all students

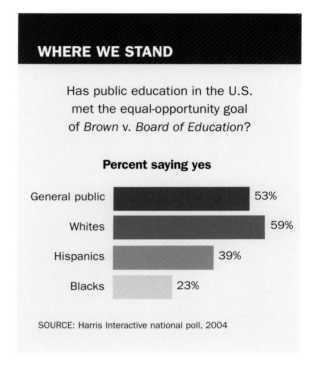

WHERE WE STAND

Has public education in the U.S. met the equal-opportunity goal of *Brown* v. *Board of Education*?

Percent saying yes

General public — 53%
Whites — 59%
Hispanics — 39%
Blacks — 23%

SOURCE: Harris Interactive national poll, 2004

have equal educational opportunities, 39 percent of the Hispanic respondents and only 23 percent of the African-American respondents agreed. The poll had a margin of error of 2 percentage points.

View on Test Gap

Attending classes, socializing, and participating in after-school activities with students of various racial and ethnic backgrounds was important to more than 90 percent of the teachers and more than 80 percent of the students questioned in the *Education Week* survey.

Both teachers and students were asked to rank the factors that they believe contribute to the "achievement gap," which finds black and Hispanic

STUDENT CONFLICTS

Compared to teachers, students are almost twice as likely to report that they "often" or "sometimes" hear or see conflicts between students of different races in school.

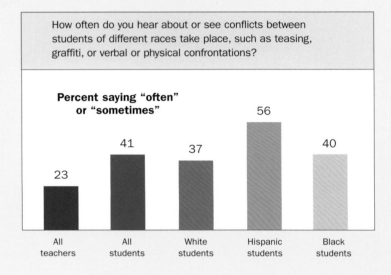

How often do you hear about or see conflicts between students of different races take place, such as teasing, graffiti, or verbal or physical confrontations?

Percent saying "often" or "sometimes"

All teachers	All students	White students	Hispanic students	Black students
23	41	37	56	40

STUDENT DISCIPLINE

Black teachers are more than seven times more likely than white teachers to think black or Hispanic students are unfairly disciplined. Students are more likely than teachers, in general, to perceive differences in how discipline is administered to students of different races.

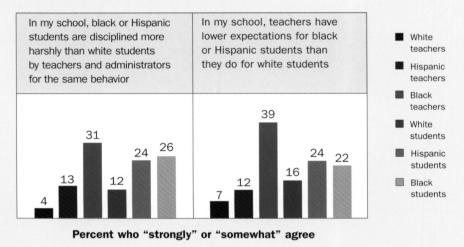

In my school, black or Hispanic students are disciplined more harshly than white students by teachers and administrators for the same behavior

In my school, teachers have lower expectations for black or Hispanic students than they do for white students

- White teachers
- Hispanic teachers
- Black teachers
- White students
- Hispanic students
- Black students

Left group: 4, 13, 31, 12, 24, 26
Right group: 7, 12, 39, 16, 24, 22

Percent who "strongly" or "somewhat" agree

REASONS FOR THE ACHIEVEMENT GAP

Almost all teachers agree that challenging family conditions and lack of family involvement explain a "great deal" or "some" of the achievement gap. But black teachers are more likely than white teachers to say school or societal factors are important explanations for the achievement gap.

Percent saying factor explains "a great deal" or "some" of the gap

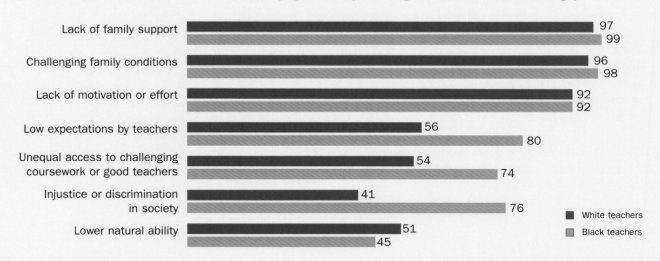

Factor	White teachers	Black teachers
Lack of family support	97	99
Challenging family conditions	96	98
Lack of motivation or effort	92	92
Low expectations by teachers	56	80
Unequal access to challenging coursework or good teachers	54	74
Injustice or discrimination in society	41	76
Lower natural ability	51	45

- White teachers
- Black teachers

SOURCE: *Education Week*, national survey of public school teachers and students on race and education, 2004

STUDENTS TALK ABOUT RACE

About half of students report that they "often" or "sometimes" talk about race relations in society during class. About one-third say they "often" or "sometimes" talk about race relations within their schools during class.

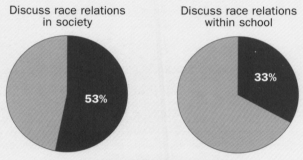

Discuss race relations in society — **53%**

Discuss race relations within school — **33%**

Percent saying "often" or "sometimes"

Among students who report such discussions, about a third of white students, compared with almost half of black students and a majority of Hispanic students, say such discussions had an effect on their thinking.

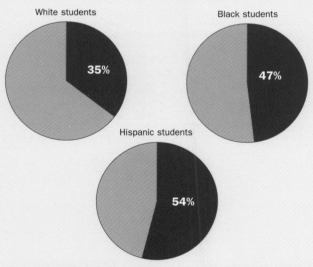

White students — **35%**

Black students — **47%**

Hispanic students — **54%**

Percent saying discussion had "a great deal" or "some" effect on understanding or opinions of different races

DOES DIVERSITY MATTER?

About three-quarters of teachers, but far fewer students, say it is "very important" for students of different races to attend school or attend classes together. Fewer than half of white students say diversity in school or in classes is very important.

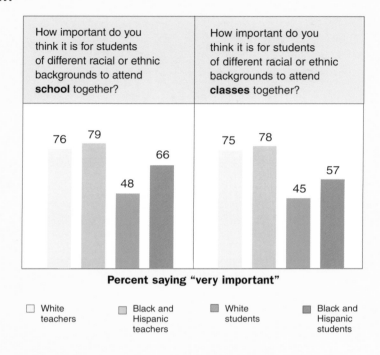

How important do you think it is for students of different racial or ethnic backgrounds to attend **school** together?

76   79   48   66

How important do you think it is for students of different racial or ethnic backgrounds to attend **classes** together?

75   78   45   57

Percent saying "very important"

☐ White teachers   ◼ Black and Hispanic teachers   ◼ White students   ◼ Black and Hispanic students

More than half of white teachers don't think racial diversity helps improve student achievement. More than three-quarters of white and Hispanic students, and a majority of black students, say having students of different races and ethnicities attend school and class together has no impact on achievement.

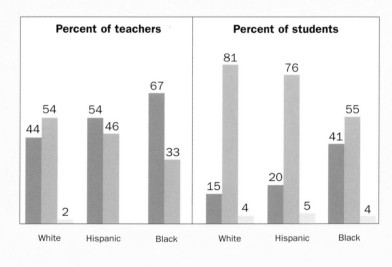

Percent of teachers

White: 44   54   2
Hispanic: 54   46
Black: 67   33

Percent of students

White: 15   81   4
Hispanic: 20   76   5
Black: 41   55   4

◼ Racial diversity makes achievement "much better" or "better"   ◼ Racial diversity makes "no difference" in achievement   ☐ Racial diversity makes achievement "much worse" or "worse"

In general, students of different races and ethnicities appear optimistic about their schools, their teachers, and how well they are being prepared for college.

But teachers in high-minority and high-poverty schools are less likely than teachers in low-poverty and low-minority schools to rate teachers, parent support, the environment for learning, and the quality of education as excellent.

**Percent of students who "strongly"
or "somewhat" agree**

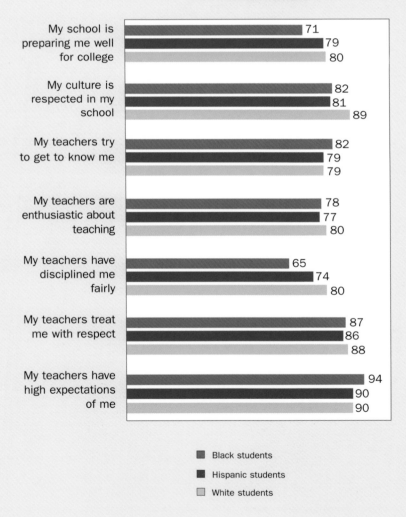

My school is preparing me well for college
- 71
- 79
- 80

My culture is respected in my school
- 82
- 81
- 89

My teachers try to get to know me
- 82
- 79
- 79

My teachers are enthusiastic about teaching
- 78
- 77
- 80

My teachers have disciplined me fairly
- 65
- 74
- 80

My teachers treat me with respect
- 87
- 86
- 88

My teachers have high expectations of me
- 94
- 90
- 90

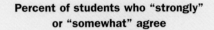

■ Black students
■ Hispanic students
□ White students

**Percent of teachers rating their school
as "excellent" on ...**

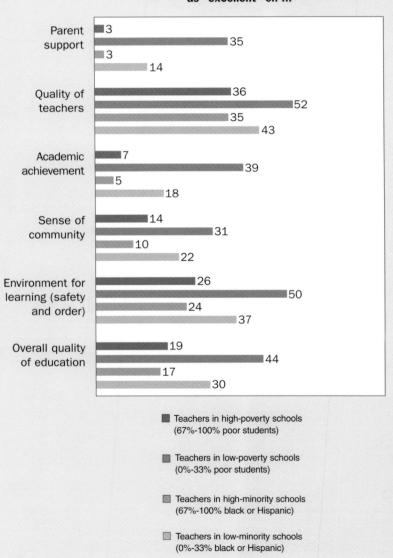

Parent support
- 3
- 35
- 3
- 14

Quality of teachers
- 36
- 52
- 35
- 43

Academic achievement
- 7
- 39
- 5
- 18

Sense of community
- 14
- 31
- 10
- 22

Environment for learning (safety and order)
- 26
- 50
- 24
- 37

Overall quality of education
- 19
- 44
- 17
- 30

■ Teachers in high-poverty schools (67%-100% poor students)

■ Teachers in low-poverty schools (0%-33% poor students)

■ Teachers in high-minority schools (67%-100% black or Hispanic)

□ Teachers in low-minority schools (0%-33% black or Hispanic)

SOURCE: *Education Week*, national survey of public school teachers and students on race and education, 2004

Public school teachers and students believe integrated schooling is important, but many don't think it affects how much students learn.

students posting lower test scores than their white and Asian counterparts. Teachers were more apt to attribute the gap to family- or student-centered factors. Overwhelming majorities pointed to lack of family support or involvement, challenging family conditions, and lack of student motivation or effort as reasons for the gap.

Black and Hispanic teachers however, were more likely than white teachers to identify low teacher expectations and "injustice or discrimination" as contributing factors. Black teachers also cited unequal access to challenging coursework and good teachers as a reason the gap exists more often than their white and Hispanic colleagues did.

Students were more inclined than teachers to identify school-related causes as explaining a great deal or some of the achievement gap. While 67 percent of students noted unequal access to challenging coursework and good teachers, 55 percent of all teachers selected that factor. But 57 percent of students cited "injustice or discrimination" in society as an explanation, compared with 44 percent of teachers.

When asked how the achievement gap could be closed, a large majority of teachers (85 percent) recommended increased parent involvement. Sixty-three percent argued that boosting student effort and motivation also would eradicate the test-score disparities.

Few teachers said that school remedies, such as giving more money to schools serving greater numbers of disadvantaged students (26 percent)

and making sure students at risk of failure have good teachers (20 percent), would bridge the learning gap.

The survey also turned up differences between teachers and students on questions about their perceptions of race relations in their schools.

Students Less Upbeat

Overall, students appeared to hold less promising views of racial interactions, with 28 percent of the students surveyed rating relations between students of different races as "excellent," compared with 34 percent of teachers. While 23 percent of teachers reported "often or sometimes" hearing or seeing conflicts between students of different races, including fights, 40 percent of students acknowledged often or sometimes witnessing such behavior.

When it comes to cross-racial relationships, more students (70 percent) than teachers (54 percent) agreed that students who share similar racial backgrounds "stick together" in school. Students reported that interaction between students of various racial backgrounds occurs less often than teachers said it did. For example, 83 percent of teachers said cross-racial interaction occurs "often" during classes, while just 60 percent of the students agreed.

Asked whether teachers have lower expectations for black and Hispanic students, 18 percent of students and 10 percent of teachers said that was the case.

Students were more likely than teachers to say that black and Hispanic students are disciplined more harshly than white students for the same behavior. But just 17 percent of students and 6 percent of teachers said so, meaning that large majorities of both groups responded that minority students aren't singled out for tougher punishments.

In fact, overwhelming majorities of teachers and students, 91 percent and 81 percent respectively, said that regardless of race or economic background, all students are treated fairly by teachers and administrators.

'Hard Issues'

Education experts who were asked to comment on the poll's findings sounded one common theme: the need for better teacher training.

As more white teachers work in schools with racially diverse student populations, cultural barriers can emerge that can lead to "conflicts and disharmony," said Lois Harrison-Jones, an associate clinical professor at Howard University in Washington and a former superintendent of the Boston public schools.

More must be done to prepare teachers—before they enter the classroom—to teach in increasingly heterogeneous environments, she said.

"Teachers need to understand and look at their own practices to make sure they're not engaging in activities or behaviors that are a detriment to one group of students," agreed Nat LaCour, the executive vice president of the American

Teachers and students, black and white, have different perceptions of the extent to which students of different races interact in and out of class.

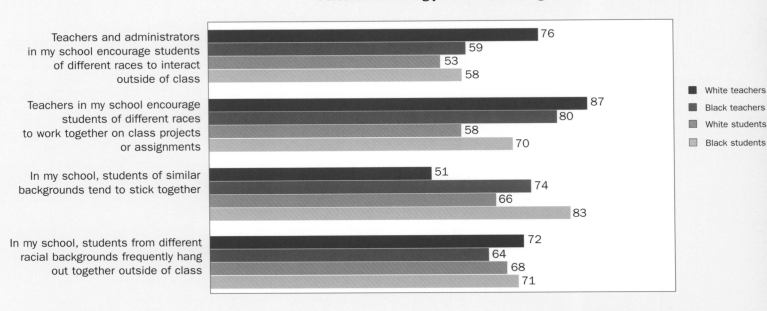

Percent who "strongly" or "somewhat" agree

Teachers and administrators in my school encourage students of different races to interact outside of class
- 76
- 59
- 53
- 58

Teachers in my school encourage students of different races to work together on class projects or assignments
- 87
- 80
- 58
- 70

In my school, students of similar backgrounds tend to stick together
- 51
- 74
- 66
- 83

In my school, students from different racial backgrounds frequently hang out together outside of class
- 72
- 64
- 68
- 71

- ■ White teachers
- ■ Black teachers
- ▨ White students
- ▨ Black students

While more than three-quarters of students say they hear bad things or jokes about different races, the vast majority do not feel uncomfortable around people of different races.

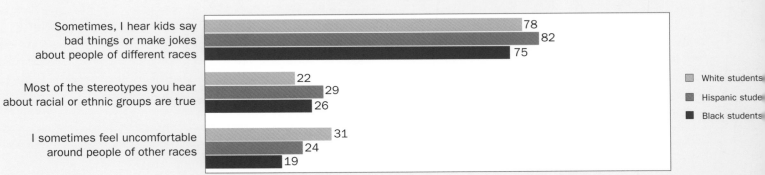

Percent who "strongly" or "somewhat" agree

Sometimes, I hear kids say bad things or make jokes about people of different races
- 78
- 82
- 75

Most of the stereotypes you hear about racial or ethnic groups are true
- 22
- 29
- 26

I sometimes feel uncomfortable around people of other races
- 31
- 24
- 19

- ▨ White students
- ▨ Hispanic stude
- ■ Black students

SOURCE: *Education Week*, national survey of public school teachers and students on race and education, 2004

Students tend to hold less promising views of racial interactions than teachers, saying that pupils of similar backgrounds "stick together."

Federation of Teachers.

The differences between teachers' and students' perceptions of racial interaction in schools were not surprising to Rossi Ray-Taylor, the executive director of the Minority Student Achievement Network, an Evanston, Ill.-based coalition of districts working to close racial and ethnic gaps in achievement.

Teachers tend to observe superficial interactions—such as whom students talk to in class, she said. But students, she said, are seeking a deeper level of interaction: "Who hangs out with who? Who's dating who?"

For teachers to point to more parental participation in schools as the solution to the achievement gap, she cautioned, is looking at education too narrowly. To Ms. Ray-Taylor, "parent involvement" has become a cliché.

"We're avoiding the hard issues of what we can do differently in classrooms and schools," she said. "Not that we should ignore poverty or segregated housing. But those realities cannot get in the way of what schools have to do."

Eric J. Cooper, the president of the Washington-based National Urban Alliance for Effective Education, which focuses on training teachers to improve urban schools, said teachers are "often unaware of the stereotypes they place on students."

"Inadvertently, [teachers] are creating a self-fulfilling prophecy that gets [minority] students to believe that they're not really capable," he said.

The rejection by majorities of teachers and students of the idea that racially diverse classes positively affect student achievement seems to conflict with their support for integrated schools, though teachers were only narrowly divided on the question.

Willis D. Hawley, a professor emeritus of education at the University of Maryland College Park, said the responses discounting such an effect could be an adverse reaction to a seemingly inappropriate statement.

Few people would espouse the belief that minority students get smarter simply by sitting next to white students, he said. Instead, one of the ways people learn is by comparing different perspectives on a given problem. In a classroom mixing students from different racial backgrounds, in Mr. Hawley's view, learning is more nuanced.

"So much of our learning is impeded by stereotypes about race and class," he added.

The attitude that diverse classes don't help student achievement dismayed Raul Gonzalez, the legislative director for the National Council of La Raza, a Washington-based advocacy group for Hispanics.

"We've given up on the idea that diversity is valuable," he said. "We tried busing. We tried magnet schools. Now we've run out of ideas. The value of diversity is not measured necessarily by reading and math scores. It's part of creating the strongest citizenry we can possibly have."

But Todd F. Gaziano, the director of the center for legal and judicial studies at the Heritage Foundation, a Washington think tank, argued that as long as legally sanctioned discrimination is eliminated, few people are concerned with school integration.

"Too much time is wasted on calculating the metrics of racial balance in the classroom," he said, "when what really matters is whether the schools are any good that parents without independent means have to send their kids to."

Wendy D. Puriefoy, the president of the Public Education Network, a Washington-based coalition of local education funds, argued that the *Brown* decision was not about integration, but about ending legal segregation.

Schools were asked to pick up the charge of integration, she said, "without the rest of society doing anything at all. I think it's an undue burden." ∎

About This Poll

Harris Interactive, a worldwide market-research and consulting firm (www.harrisinteractive.com) based in Rochester, N.Y., and best known for the Harris Poll, conducted *Education Week*'s national survey of public school teachers and students on race and education.

Harris Interactive conducted online interviews with 2,591 K-12 public school teachers from Feb. 12 to March 8, 2004. Teacher data were weighted to be representative of all U.S. K-12 public school teachers. Another online survey of 1,102 public school students in grades 7-12 was conducted from Feb. 24 to March 8, and those data were weighted to be representative of all U.S. public school students in grades 7-12.

The margin of sampling error on the teacher poll is plus or minus 2.6 percentage points. The margin of error on the student poll is plus or minus 4.5 percentage points.

Public Overwhelmingly Expresses Support for Diverse Classrooms

But Fewer Poll Respondents See Academic Benefits

BY KATHRYN M. DOHERTY

The 50th anniversary of the U.S. Supreme Court's decision in *Brown* v. *Board of Education of Topeka* was an opportunity for *Education Week* to survey teachers and students about the role of race in school, including their perceptions of fair treatment, friendships, classroom interactions, and academic achievement. We concluded, not surprisingly, that race still matters.

But we also wanted to take the pulse of the general public to find out how committed Americans today are to the goals of *Brown*. In the spring of 2004, *Education Week* worked with Harris Interactive, a Rochester, N.Y.,-based polling firm that conducts the well-known Harris Poll, to pose such questions to the American public.

We found that while significant lip service is paid to the importance of racial diversity in schools and classrooms, many fewer Americans believe that racial mixing is helpful to student achievement—especially for white student achievement.

Across the board, approximately 90 percent of the Americans surveyed think racial diversity and mixing in schools, classes, extracurricular

activities, and social settings is important for students. But a significantly smaller percentage of the general public thinks racial diversity in these areas is "very" important. Sixty-eight percent of Americans think it is very important for students of different races to attend class together. Sixty-two percent think it is very important for young people of different races to socialize together. White respondents are less likely than black or Hispanic respondents to think these are very important goals.

Democrats are more likely than Republicans, 75 percent to 62 percent, respectively, to think it is very important for different races to attend classes together.

Meeting the Goals of *Brown*

While just half of those polled said they were familiar with the *Brown* decision, we asked nearly 4,000 Americans to consider where public education in the United States stands on providing equal educational opportunities to minority students. Poll respondents were asked how much they agreed or disagreed with the statement "African-American or Hispanic students are just as likely as white students to get

a good education in the U.S." Overall, 60 percent of the general public "strongly" or "somewhat" agree that students of different races are just as likely to get a good education in the nation's schools.

While a majority of the public overall thinks that white and minority students have equal educational chances, white Americans are most likely to think that is true. Black opinion diverges strongly. Sixty-five percent of whites think students of different races have equal chances in the United States. Almost exactly the same proportion of African-Americans, or 64 percent, strongly or somewhat disagree that minority students are just as likely as white students to get a good education in this country.

Seventy-two percent of Republicans, compared with 49 percent of Democrats, agree that African-American and Hispanic students are just as likely as white students to get a good education in the United States.

The Harris Poll also asked Americans whether they thought public education in the United States has met the equal opportunity goal of *Brown*. Here the public, in general, appeared evenly split. Fifty-three percent of the general public think the goal of equal opportunity has been met; 47 percent think it has not. An overwhelming 77 percent of African-Americans and 61 percent of Hispanics, compared with 41 percent of whites, say the goal of equal academic opportunities for all students has not been met.

Diversity and Achievement

In principle, Americans say they value racial mixing in schools and classrooms. Large majorities of Americans from various racial, ethnic, economic, and political groups think "diversity" in schools and classrooms is important. But barely a majority of the respondents to the poll think diversity improves the quality of education for black or Hispanic students, and many fewer think it benefits white students.

White and black respondents are in relatively close agreement on how they think racial mixing affects black students: Fifty-one percent of white respondents and 58 percent of black respondents think racial diversity helps the quality of black students' education. But 21 percent of white Americans, compared with 7 percent of black respondents, think that racial mixing hurts white student performance. About a third of both white and black Americans think racial diversity has no effect on the performance of white students. Twenty-six percent of blacks believe diversity has no effect or makes student achievement worse for African-American students.

Just 50 percent of Americans think having racially integrated schools helps the achievement of low-income students. ∎

About This Poll

As part of our coverage of the 50th anniversary of the *Brown* v. *Board of Education of Topeka* decision, *Education Week* worked with Harris Interactive of Rochester, N.Y., to survey American adults' views on race and education. The responses to each question asked on the national survey are available online, including response rates specific to demographic, racial, and ethnic subgroups participating in the survey. See **www.edweek.org/sreports/brownpoll.pdf**.

The Harris Poll® was conducted online within the United States between March 18 and 29, 2004, among a nationwide cross-section of 3,698 adults. Figures for age, sex, race, education, and number of adults in the household were weighted to bring them into line with their actual proportions in the population. With probability samples of this size, one could say with 95 percent certainty that the results have a statistical precision of plus or minus 2 percentage points of what they would be if the entire adult population had been polled with complete accuracy.

African-Americans are much less likely than white or Hispanic respondents to think that minority students have equal chances at a good education in the United States.

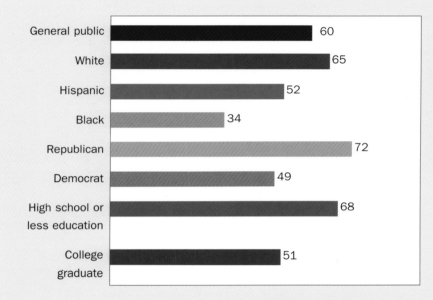

Percent of Americans who "strongly" or "somewhat" agree that African-American or Hispanic students are just as likely as white students to get a good education.

General public	60
White	65
Hispanic	52
Black	34
Republican	72
Democrat	49
High school or less education	68
College graduate	51

Percent of Americans who think it is "very important" that students of different races and ethnicities attend class together.

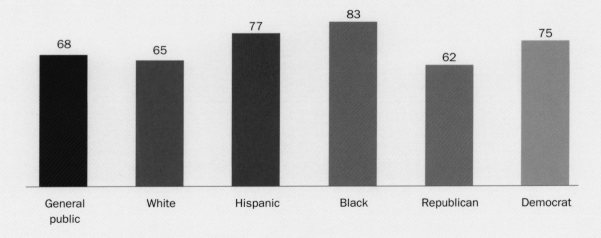

General public	White	Hispanic	Black	Republican	Democrat
68	65	77	83	62	75

SOURCE: Harris Interactive national poll, 2004

Just half of Americans believe that efforts to have students of different races attend school together benefit minority student achievement.

Percent of Americans who think racial diversity in schools improves education for ...

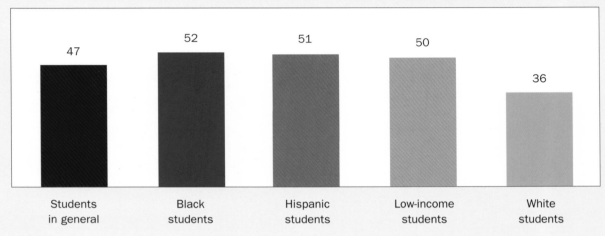

Students in general	Black students	Hispanic students	Low-income students	White students
47	52	51	50	36

African-Americans are more likely than white or Hispanic respondents to think that there are advantages to having single-race schools specifically for black students.

Percent of Americans who "strongly" or "somewhat" agree that there are advantages to having schools dedicated to educating black students only

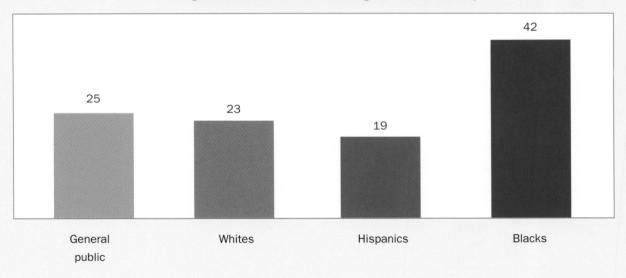

General public	Whites	Hispanics	Blacks
25	23	19	42

SOURCE: Harris Interactive national poll, 2004

African-American mother Nettie Hunt and her daughter Nickie sit on the steps of the U.S. Supreme Court shortly after the high court's ruling in the *Brown* v. *Board of Education of Topeka* case.

'A Shining Moment'

BY ABIGAIL THERNSTROM

From segregation to "resegregation": what a depressing picture. It's become the conventional wisdom, in the media and elsewhere, on what has happened to the country since the decision in *Brown* v. *Board of Education of Topeka* was handed down 50 years ago. But it is not correct. Some, like Philadelphia schools chief Paul Vallas, may say that "we're still wrestling with the same issues" as we did in 1954. Nonsense. *Brown* remains a shining moment in American history, and the changes that came in its wake can never be undone.

How quickly we forget. Fifty years ago, when *Brown* was decided, there was no interracial contact in the schools of the South, the region where most African-American children lived. Even 10 years later, in the 11 ex-Confederate states as a whole, a mere 1.2 percent of black public school children went to schools that any white pupils attended.

State-imposed pupil assignments that separated the races were what *Brown* v. *Board* was all about. The U.S. Supreme Court did not condemn—and never has—racially imbalanced schools per se. It spoke of the "detrimental effect" that officially sanctioned separation of the races had—"denoting the inferiority of the Negro group," generating "a feeling of inferiority as to their status in the community. . . ." The message was pertinent to the entire Jim Crow system, not just the rules governing education. The whole point of state-sanctioned segregation, from water fountains to hospitals, was to convey a permanent sense of racial inferiority. That purpose drove the rules governing seats on a bus, as well as those dictating school assignments. Hence the domino effect—the rapid extension of the ruling in *Brown* to other spheres of southern public life. The logic of the court's decision could not be confined to schools.

Southern apartheid crumbled—too slowly, for sure, but down a long, hard road it did fall apart. Today, the typical black child attends a school in which just over half the students are African-American, nearly a third are white, and there are sizable numbers of Latinos and Asians as well. Moreover, close to a third of blacks and a quarter of Latinos are in schools with white majorities. Gary Orfield, the director of the Civil Rights Project at Harvard University, and others who argue "resegregation" are simply counting the number of whites in a school system, and finding that number inadequate across much of the urban landscape.

That definition has an odd result. A school in Louisiana that reflects the state's population (half white, half black) is labeled as more "integrated" than one in San Francisco, where public school enrollment is currently 11 percent white, 16 percent black, 22 percent Hispanic, 0.6 percent American Indian, and 51 percent Asian. Yet surely the logic of calling a majority-Asian school with few whites "segregated"—with the implication that learning is likely to be compromised—makes no sense given the record of Asian academic accomplishment. In addition, such diversity, such a rainbow of colors, is a civil rights dream come true, one might think.

Simply counting whites also ignores the demographic landscape. The standard measure of racial separation (which Gary Orfield rejects) asks quite a different question: the degree to which schools are "imbalanced" relative to the actual racial mix in the district. The Imbalance Index—as it's called—takes the number of white students in a district as a fact, and focuses on the distribution of children, given the existing demographic constraints. By that measure, there has been much improvement over the past three decades.

A Boston school, by the measure of "imbalance," is not "segregated" when it is roughly 13 percent white because

Abigail Thernstrom is the co-author (with Stephan Thernstrom) of *No Excuses: Closing the Racial Gap in Learning*. She is also a member of the U.S. Commission on Civil Rights, a member of the Massachusetts state board of education, and a senior fellow at the Manhattan Institute.

Derrick Bell is a visiting professor of law at New York University, and was for 15 years a member of the Harvard Law School faculty. During the 1960s, as an NAACP Legal Defense and Educational Fund lawyer, he handled and supervised hundreds of school desegregation cases. This essay is adapted from his book Silent Covenants: *Brown* v. *Board of Education and the Unfulfilled Hopes for Racial Reform*, copyright © 2004 by Oxford University Press Inc., and is used by permission of Oxford University Press Inc.

'A Magnificent Mirage'

BY DERRICK BELL

Over the decades, the *Brown* decision, like other landmark cases, has gained a life quite apart from the legal questions it was intended to settle. The passage of time has calmed both the ardor of its admirers and the ire of its detractors. Today, of little use as legal precedent, it has gained in reputation as a measure of what law and society might be. That noble image, dulled by resistance to any but minimal steps toward compliance, has transformed *Brown* into a magnificent mirage, the legal equivalent of that city on a hill to which all aspire without any serious thought that it will ever be attained.

Considered within the context of American political, economic, and cultural life, the *Brown* decision is a long-running racial melodrama. As with a film or play, the decision stimulated varying feeling. It energized the law, encouraged most black people, enraged a great many white people, and, like so many other racial policies, served the nation's short-term but not its long-term interests. Generating an emotionally charged concoction of commendations and condemnations, the *Brown* decision recreated the 19th century's post-Civil War Reconstruction/Redemption pattern of progress followed by retrogression. It stirred confusion and conflict into the always-vexing question of race in a society that, despite denials and a frustratingly flexible amnesia, owes much of its growth, development, and success to the ability of those dominant members of society who use race to both control and exploit most people, whatever their race.

As had happened in the past, the law employing the vehicle of a major judicial decision offered symbolic encouragement to the black dispossessed. The substantive losses so feared by its white adversaries evolved almost unnoticed into advances greater for whites than for blacks.

And a half-century later, as must now be apparent to all, the nation's racial dilemma—modernized and, one might say, "colorized,"—has become more complex rather than simplified. The ever-widening racial disparities in all aspects of life overshadow the gains in status achieved by those black Americans who, by varying combinations of hard work and good fortune, are viewed as having "made it." Indeed, although it did not achieve what its supporters hoped for, historians and other social scientists, safely removed from the fray, may come to view *Brown* as the perfect precedent. As a dictionary would define perfect, it was: "pure, total; lacking in no essential detail; complete, sane, absolute, unequivocal, unmitigated, an act of perfection."

They will have a point. In law, perfection in the social-reform area is a legal precedent that resolves issues in a manner that: (1) initially or over time gains acceptance from broad segments of the populace; (2) protects vested property in all its forms through sanctions against generally recognized wrongdoers; (3) encourages investment, confidence, and security through a general upholding of the status quo; and (4) while recognizing severe injustices, does not disrupt the reasonable expectations of those not directly responsible for the wrongs. Such reform is arranged of seeming necessity within the context of a silent covenant. That is, the policymakers who approve the policy do so with the knowledge, unspoken but clearly understood, that they or those who follow them stand ready to modify or even withdraw the reforms where adverse reaction or changed circumstances threaten any of the first three components.

Arguably, the *Brown* decision eventually met each of these standards. The question is whether another approach than the one embraced by the *Brown* decision might have been more effective and less disruptive in the always-contentious racial arena. The claim that the perfect is the enemy of the good sounds like a bureaucratic excuse for failing to do what needs to be done. At least in the first *Brown* decision, the Supreme Court did not settle for the pragmatic approach. Overcoming fears of predictable resistance, the court sought to change society with one swift blow. A year later, the court, in *Brown II*, reacted to the outraged cries of "never" coming from the South and the absence of support from the executive and legislative branches, and backed away from its earlier commitment. In evident response to the resistance, the court issued a fall-back decision that became a prelude to its refusal to issue orders requiring any meaningful school desegregation for almost 15 years. . . .

***

Brown, then, served to reinforce the fiction that, by the decision's rejection of racial barriers posed by segregation, the path of progress would be clear. Everyone can and should make it through individual ability and effort. One would have thought that this reinforcement of the status quo would placate if not please even the strongest supporters of segregation. To the contrary, the *Brown* decision provided politicians with a racial issue with which to enrage and upset large groups of white people, initially in the South, but far more generally as efforts to implement the decision moved across the country.

In effect, they demanded the name of segregation as well as the game of racial preference. Courts initially responded to this

whites are only 13 percent of the city's school population. The charge of "segregation" would seem to suggest a problem that has a remedy. But no amount of goodwill can change the fact that in central cities, especially, the number of blacks, Hispanics, and Asians has grown substantially in recent decades, and thus the proportion of white students has gone down. School districts cannot change their racial makeup, and the sorry history of busing (with no gains in student achievement) suggests schools should concentrate on good education for the children who appear on their doorstep, however racially "imbalanced" that group of pupils might be.

The end of de jure segregation in the South did not level the educational playing field. The Supreme Court in 1954 only raised such hopes implicitly, however. The decision was almost a blank slate, more notable for what it omitted than for what it actually said. The wait from *Plessy* v. *Ferguson* to *Brown* had been so long that inevitably Americans who were committed to civil rights read their hopes of true racial equality into the sparse opinion. But the '54 decision was only a minimal response to morally and constitutionally egregious wrongs.

That minimal response contained no reference to a colorblind Constitution. In 1896, Justice John Marshall Harlan, dissenting in *Plessy*, had argued that "our Constitution is colorblind, and neither knows nor tolerates classes among citizens." But that wonderful dissent was the radical vision of a man who has remained a voice in the constitutional wilderness. *Brown* contained no singing phrases, no majestic moral rhetoric. Its conclusion was clear enough, but the

An African-American child does not need to sit next to a white student to become a good reader—any more that a white youngster needs to sit next to an Asian to learn math.

substance was not. And thus the decision was left vulnerable to a process of revision that, over time, legitimized race-conscious strategies in an effort to achieve racially balanced schools— strategies that the attorneys for the plaintiffs in *Brown* had explicitly rejected. In fact, a few years after the '54 decision, one of Thurgood Marshall's chief legal aides, Jack Greenberg, declared that if there were "complete freedom of choice, or geographical zoning, or any other nonracial standard, and all the Negroes still ended up in separate schools, there would seem to be no constitutional objection."

Race-conscious strategies like busing were driven by the desire for better schooling. Integration was essential to learning, busing advocates insisted. But, while the Detroit school district is almost entirely black, that is no excuse for the failure to impart the skills and knowledge that those students need to do well in American society. Equal educational outcomes for the typical child in every racial and ethnic group should be the first aim of American educators today. Racial equality depends on it. The focus on "resegregation" is a distraction from that task. An African-American child does not need to sit next to a white student to become a good reader—any more than a white youngster needs resistance with caution intended to give time for the process to work, and later with a series of stronger and more specific orders intended as much to uphold judicial authority as to effectively carry out the mandate of *Brown*. These orders were carried out eventually, but the fear of sending their children to desegregated schools led many white parents either to move to mainly white school districts or to enroll their children in private, all-white schools. With their departure went the primary reason for racial-balance remedies. ...

Landmark decisions are, at bottom, designed through reference to constitutional interpretations and supportive legal precedents to address and hopefully resolve deeply divisive social issues. They are framed in a language that provides at least the appearance of doing justice without unduly upsetting large groups whose potential for noncompliance can frustrate relief efforts and undermine judicial authority. For reasons that may not even have been apparent to the members of the Supreme Court, their school desegregation decisions achieved over time a far loftier place in legal history than they were able to accomplish in reforming the ideology of racial domination that *Plessy* v. *Ferguson* represented.

Brown teaches that advocates of racial justice should rely less on judicial decisions and more on tactics, actions, and even attitudes that challenge the continuing assumptions of white dominance. History as well as current events call for realism in our racial dealings. Traditional statements of freedom and justice for all, the usual fare on celebratory occasions, serve to mask

> *Brown* teaches that advocates of racial justice should rely less on judicial decisions and more on tactics, actions, and even attitudes that challenge the continuing assumptions of white dominance.

continuing manifestations of inequality that beset and divide people along lines of color and class. These divisions have been exploited to enable an uneasy social stability, but at a cost that is not less onerous because it is all too obvious to blacks and all but invisible to a great many whites. . . .

The landscape for meaningful racial reform is neither smooth nor easily traveled. History's lessons have not been learned, and even at this late date may not be teachable. Racial reforms that blacks view as important are opposed by many whites as a threat to their status, an unfair effort to make them pay for wrongs that neither they nor their families have committed. Color blindness, now as a century ago, is adopted as the easy resolution of issues of race with which the nation would rather not wrestle, much less try seriously to resolve. It is an attractive veneer obscuring flaws in the society that are not corrected by being hidden from view. *Brown* v. *Board of Education* was a dramatic instance of a remedy that promised to correct deficiencies in justice far deeper than the Supreme Court was able to understand. ∎

to sit next to an Asian to learn math.

The average black or Hispanic student today leaves high school with an 8th grade education. On the nation's most reliable tests—the National Assessment of Educational Progress—the typical non-Asian minority student at age 17 is scoring less well than at least 80 percent of his or her white classmates. In fact, in five of the seven subjects tested by NAEP, a majority of black students perform in the lowest category—"below basic." These students do not have even a "partial" mastery of the "fundamental" knowledge and skills expected of students in the 12th grade. Hispanics are doing only a tad better. Moreover, the news is no happier when we switch our gaze to the top of the scale. In math, for instance, only 0.2 percent of black students fall into NAEP's "advanced" category; the figure for whites is 11 times higher and for Asians 37 times higher. Again, Hispanic students are only slightly ahead of blacks.

This is the problem that *Brown* could not fix—although of course it was much worse a half-century ago. But for more than a decade, scores have been stagnant, and a further closing of the racial gap in learning will likely take profound educational change.

'Figuring out what constitutes good schooling—the sort that would really make for equal educational opportunity—is not hard. But no one has a good answer to the question of how to put such education in place across the nation, wherever kids are failing to get the skills and knowledge they desperately need to do well in today's America. Ensuring skills and knowledge—not somehow finding more white classmates for minority students—is the unfinished business of *Brown*. It could not be more urgent. ∎

Still Standing in the Schoolhouse Door

BY JACQUELINE JORDAN IRVINE

Jacqueline Jordan Irvine is the Charles Howard Candler professor of urban education at Emory University, in Atlanta.

When the *Brown* decision was handed down 50 years ago, there was celebration and escalated hopes and dreams for all who believed in and loved freedom and democracy. Many thought that, at last, black and white children would attend schools together, become friends, and grow into enlightened citizens, and that the walls of segregation, racism, and prejudice would come tumbling down. More importantly, the visionaries and architects of *Brown* thought that desegregation of public schools would have a domino effect, and that other barriers in housing, employment, and higher education would collapse. When the decision was rendered, the future U.S. Supreme Court Justice Thurgood Marshall, who worked arduously for 20 years to dismantle segregation, said, "We hit the jackpot." Later he recalled, "I was so happy I was numb." Although Marshall and the NAACP admitted that there was much work yet to be accomplished in implementing *Brown,* he told a reporter in 1954 that school segregation would be eliminated nationwide within five years.

Unfortunately, those dreams of equal opportunity were not to be fully realized because dream-breakers literally stood in the schoolhouse door. The icon seared into our consciousness is the image of Gov. George C. Wallace of Alabama. His defiance, hatred, and obstinate racist positions are indelibly etched in my own mind. On June 11, 1963, I was 200 miles away as Gov. Wallace made his stand at the University of Alabama and reaffirmed his proclamation made at his inauguration: "Segregation now. Segregation tomorrow. Segregation forever."

Fortunately, George Wallace and people like him are no longer physically standing in schoolhouse doors. Yet there are dream-breakers, reminiscent of Wallace, who are still among us. The mandate to proceed with "all deliberate speed" has stalled, and the dream of equal educational opportunity even now appears elusive. Two factors, I believe, represent the greatest disappointments of *Brown*: the increase in segregation in schools, and the continuing decline in the school achievement of African-American and Latino students.

The Civil Rights Project at Harvard University and the Educational Testing Service provide some sobering statistics on desegregation. Segregation has been on the rise in the last decade, despite rapid increases in the number of students of color. U.S. Census Bureau data indicate that the white population in the United States is declining, while 40 percent of the students in our schools come from ethnically diverse backgrounds. However, this growing diversity does not foretell growing integration. The average white student attends a school that is 80 percent white. The average African-American student attends a school that is 67 percent African-American. The most segregated of all minority groups are Latinos. Seventy-five percent of Latinos attend mostly minority schools. Adding to the complexity of this picture is the fact that not only are these schools segregated, but also the students of color who attend them are overwhelmingly poor.

That our schools are still segregated is disturbing enough. More troubling is the fact that far too many African-American and Latino students in these mostly segregated schools are performing poorly. One of the most trenchant areas of concern among educators and researchers is the test-score gap, or the general tendency for white and Asian students to score higher on standardized measures of achievement than their black and Hispanic peers.

This test-score gap is revealed in the fact that white students, on average, score 20 to 30 points higher than their black and Hispanic peers. But the importance of the discrepancy becomes even more apparent when considering what a 30-point difference

Political Leaders are now playing a horrible shell game with the lives of poor and minority students, and have eliminated or underfunded most federal legislative and judicial efforts aimed at decreasing segregation and the achievement gap.

means for the average black or Hispanic student. Seventeen-year-old black and Hispanic students have skills in reading, mathematics, and science that are similar to those of a 13-year old white student.

Credible research has documented variables that explain why students of color in mostly segregated schools continue to fall behind their white and Asian peers. Residential segregation, supported by decades of reversals of school busing cases, has contributed to hypersegregation, particularly in medium to large urban areas. Housing patterns are not the sole explanation, however. As census data reveal, the suburbs are now over one-fourth minority. The other contributing factor to school segregation is the increase in private school enrollment by white students. White private school enrollment in 2000 was comparable to that in 1968.

The ETS recently published the results of a review of thousands of pieces of empirical research in an effort to determine what we know about achieving a quality education for all children. The researchers identified 14 correlates of achievement that they claim are "unambiguous," including, for example, highly qualified and experienced teachers; a challenging, academic curriculum; safe and well-funded schools; involved parents; prenatal care; preschool literacy experiences; and a decrease in the number of female-headed households.

None of these factors should come as a surprise. We have known about the salience of these issues since President Lyndon B. Johnson's Great Society and War on Poverty programs in the 1960s. Why have we, as a nation, ignored them? Why were the promises of *Brown* never fully realized? Who or what is standing in the schoolhouse door today? I contend that the most disturbing dream-breaker of *Brown* is the lack of moral leadership in this country, particularly at the national level. Although the federal government has no legal or constitutional responsibility for educational issues, the fact of the matter is that the federal government, and particularly the courts, have always been the dream-keepers for generations of Americans in search of equal opportunities.

Political leaders are now playing a horrible shell game with the lives of poor and minority students, and have eliminated or underfunded most federal legislative and judicial efforts aimed at decreasing segregation and the achievement gap. The No Child Left Behind Act is a prime example of the national public relations strategy that uses children as political pawns. When taken at its face value, the law looks promising. Who would take offense at a mandate requiring states to be accountable for the achievement of poor students, special-needs students, and students of color?

On closer review, however, critics have unveiled a disingenuous law that pledges to raise 100 percent of all students to proficient levels in reading and math by 2014, without any attention to fully funding the law or providing other needed assistance to children and their families in areas such as health care, employment, and pre- and after-school care. The No Child Left Behind law ignores the best practices of measurement and evaluation, and makes a mockery of the definition of a "highly qualified teacher." States can define the criteria for a qualified teacher. In my own state of Georgia, anyone with a bachelor's degree who passes Praxis tests in basic skills, subject matter, and principles of teaching and learning can teach. No college training in education or field experience is required. Texas has passed a similar plan.

Such inadequately prepared teachers will not be found in the suburban schools of middle-class students. They will be in the schools with the most vacancies—segregated rural and urban schools with large numbers of low-income minority students. If, after several years of trial and error and on-the-job training, these novice teachers become effective and accomplished, the data suggest they will leave their poor, urban, or rural schools and transfer to more lucrative and less challenging assignments.

We will not and cannot achieve our national vision by ignoring children with broken dreams and broken promises. Somehow, we must start to think of our future as inextricably linked to the success of poor and minority students, who remain the dispossessed heirs of Jim Crow. Fifty years after *Brown*, it's clear that we have the knowledge, skills, and technology to make the promises of that landmark ruling a reality. What we lack are visionary and courageous leaders with generous hearts.

Ron Edmonds, the trailblazer of the school reform movement, noted 35 years ago that we already know all we need to know to provide a quality education for all children. "Whether we do or do not," he said, "depends upon how we feel about the fact that we have not done it." ∎

The Legacy of 'All Deliberate Speed'

BY PEDRO A. NOGUERA & ROBERT COHEN

How should the nation commemorate the 50th anniversary of the U.S. Supreme Court's decision in *Brown* v. *Board of Education of Topeka*? We could celebrate this historic decision for outlawing apartheid in public education and establishing a precedent for ending racial segregation in other areas of American society. Or, perhaps more realistically, we could reflect upon the court's vagueness about enforcing this decision—its offering the odd term "all deliberate speed" in place of a real timetable for school desegregation. With this phrasing, we can see that imprecision as the first of many evasions that even liberal whites made when it came to translating *Brown* into educational policy.

The legacy of this history of avoidance and delay has left our public schools so segregated (though on a de facto rather than de jure basis) that there are good grounds for questioning whether there is much to celebrate on *Brown*'s 50th. New York City's public schools serve as an excellent example. At first glance, they appear to be among the most diverse in the world. Over 100 different languages and cultures are represented among the 1.1 million students, and over a third of those students are either foreign-born or the children of newly arrived immigrants.

But a closer look reveals that the ghost of Jim Crow lingers even amidst this multicultural mosaic. More than 73 percent of the city's schools are virtually segregated. Approximately 900 schools have student populations that are 80 percent to 100 percent African-American, Latino, or both. The schools are segregated by income as well as race. In the vast majority of these schools, more than 85 percent of the students qualify for free or reduced-priced lunches. Although over 40 percent of New Yorkers are white, only 15.3 percent of the students enrolled in the city's public schools are U.S.-born whites.

Much of America shares with New York this pattern of profound race and class isolation. Even the sites of some of the most famous victories for school desegregation, such as Little Rock, Ark.'s Central High School, have, because of white flight, re-segregated. In the 1990s, the proportion of black students attending all-minority schools rose from 33 percent to 37 percent, and in the South the proportion of black students enrolled in white-majority schools plummeted from 44 percent to 33 percent. Disturbingly, Latinos, who now make up the fastest-growing ethnic group in the nation, are now more likely to be segregated than any other group.

Unlike 50 years ago, when there was a growing sense that racial integration was a moral goal worth pursuing, today that optimism has vanished, and segregation in our schools and elsewhere is accepted as an unavoidable feature of life in America.

The president's No Child Left Behind law contains no plan to support racial integration or to further equity among poor and affluent schools. Even Democrats and other liberal critics of this law have said nothing about its failure to deal with the persistence and expansion of de facto segregation in America's schools. Thus, one way to truly honor *Brown* may be to challenge the left and right sides of the American educational debate to stop running away from the issue of school segregation.

A second way to commemorate *Brown* would be to honor those few school districts that are still trying to make school desegregation work, such as the 21 districts in the Minority Student Achievement Network. These districts have defied national trends and remain racially and socioeconomically integrated. Though challenged by a variety of equity issues and a persistent achievement gap, such districts serve as an example of what might have been if we had had the leadership and resolve to realize the goals of *Brown*. Though far from perfect, such districts show us that one of the most

Pedro A. Noguera (top), an urban sociologist, and Robert Cohen, a historian, are professors at New York University's Steinhardt school of education, in New York City.

The American Dilemma Continues

Sheryll Cashin
is the author of
*The Failures of
Integration: How Race
and Class
Are Undermining
the American Dream*
(PublicAffairs, 2004),
from which she
adapted this essay.
A professor of law
at Georgetown
University, she was
a law clerk to U.S.
Supreme Court Justice
Thurgood Marshall.

BY SHERYLL CASHIN

Public schools became more segregated in the 1990s. More so than our neighborhoods, our schools are bastions of race and class privilege on the one hand, and race and class disadvantage on the other. Everyone in America, from President Bush to the average parent of whatever race, intrinsically understands this. It is an unspoken truth that we do not own up to: America's schools are separate and unequal.

In any given metropolitan area, I could tell a tale of two different schools, a tale in which inequality closely mirrors the race and class of the students attending the school. Parents know these dichotomies all too well. Many, if not most, white parents stake their decisions about where to live and where to send their kids to school on such inequality—that is, they assiduously avoid the "bad" schools, which typically are minority and/or heavily poor, and they work overtime to get their children into the "good" schools, which typically are predominantly white and middle class.

In the Washington metropolitan area, where I live, an idyllic suburban high school like Walt Whitman High in Bethesda, Md., stands in stark contrast to Ballou Senior High School, located in Congress Heights in the District of Columbia's poorest ward. Whitman is high-achieving, 78 percent white, and only 1 percent to 2 percent poor. Ballou is low-achieving, 99.9 percent African-American, and 87 percent poor. Recently, fewer than 5 percent of Ballou students performed at the level of "proficient" on Stanford-9 tests in math and reading. The current school year has been hellish. In addition to being closed for a month in the fall when someone took mercury from a science classroom and spread it around the building, Ballou has been plagued by fits of

violence. The latest of several fistfights that have broken out among students involving loosely organized gangs turned deadly. Thomas Boykin fatally shot another student, James Richardson, a star football player, near the school cafeteria. The children of Ballou deserve a shot at the first-class quality of education Whitman students receive. Yet their racial and economic isolation translates into a reality that would make most of us shudder were we forced to endure it.

The *Brown* decision represents an idea that is fundamental to our democratic values. It reimagined Thomas Jefferson's vision of common schools: the idea that there should be at least one institution in American society that provides a common experience of citizenship and equal opportunity, regardless of the lottery of birth, on a free and open basis to all. Clearly we have failed to live up to *Brown*; we are not even living up to the repugnant principle announced in *Plessy* v. *Ferguson* in 1896. Our schools are separate, but hardly equal.

As of 2000, seven out of 10 black and Latino students attended predominantly minority schools, and eight out of 10 white students attended predominantly white schools. The average black or Latino student attends classes where almost half of his peers are poor. The average white student, on the other hand, attends a school where less than one in five of his peers is classified as poor. Asian students come closest to the integrationist ideal; they are most apt to be in a school that is both middle-class and multiracial.

When you place most black and Latino kids in majority-minority and heavily-poor schools, there are two main consequences, both of which contribute to an achievement gap. First, because poor students typically have greater needs, schools composed of poor students are costlier to run than schools composed of middle- and upper-income students. But in a segregated landscape where property-tax wealth is concentrated elsewhere, these extra costs are rarely covered in a way that can make a difference—that is, with small class sizes and excellent teachers. With national teacher shortages, very few strong teachers are opting to teach in challenging, often dangerous high-poverty schools that offer less pay than that available from more advantaged school systems. Second, students in schools with large numbers of poor students risk falling prey to an oppositional culture that often denigrates learning—one where pursuit of academic excellence is often perceived as "acting white." They do not enjoy a wealth of activist parents who model success and can work the educational system. White students, on the other hand, largely attend school in predominantly middle-class environments and therefore experience a very different culture—one oriented toward achievement.

The latest federal approach is not helping much. The Bush administration's No Child Left Behind Act responds to the achievement dilemma in part by requiring standards testing for all racial groups and mandating penalties for failing schools. But the act is heavier on mandates for testing than it is with additional

One way to truly honor *Brown* may be to challenge the left and right sides of the American educational debate to stop running away from the issue of school segregation.

important benefits of integration is the presence of middle-class parents who utilize their political clout to advocate for resources that benefit all students, and students who are better prepared to handle the challenges of living in a diverse society because of the education they received.

We can also honor *Brown* by revisiting the issue of integration in communities of color. Many black and Latino communities gave up long ago on school integration because of white resistance to busing. In many cases, desegregation also resulted in the closure of schools in black and brown communities and the loss of African-American teachers. As a result of these unintended consequences of *Brown*, many communities of color are increasingly focusing on how to make our racially separate schools more equal. That focus has yielded a small number of successful, selective public schools that cater primarily to black and Latino students. Schools such as Fredrick Douglass Academy in Harlem and the Young Women's Leadership School in Manhattan demonstrate that it is possible to create educational institutions that produce high levels of achievement for students of color in racially segregated settings, when adequate resources are provided.

The success of such schools also suggests that, for the time being, the best hope for many minority children may be to accept racial segregation and do what we can to create more high-quality segregated schools. While this may be the most pragmatic thing to do, we must also recognize how our sights have been lowered as we return to the unfulfilled "separate but equal" promise of *Plessy* v. *Ferguson*, the fatally flawed, segregationist U.S. Supreme Court decision that *Brown* overturned.

Throughout the country, the more common experience for students is to attend schools that are separate and unequal—schools that are well-equipped and cater to the children of the affluent, and schools that barely function and serve the poor, white and nonwhite. Throughout America, a majority of poor children attend schools where learning has been reduced to preparation for a standardized test, where failure and dropping out are accepted as the norm, and where overcrowding and disorder are common. Those who believe that integration remains a goal worth pursuing must recognize that no law can force middle-class whites to enroll their children in schools they seek to avoid, either because they are too black or simply too bad, for the sake of integration.

So perhaps the best way to honor *Brown* is to use it to recast the current debate over school reform. Let's stop seeing reform as an end in itself and start asking how improved schools in all communities can be used to attract multiracial student enrollments to those schools. And let's start demanding that *Brown*'s vision of integrated schools be addressed by politicians of both major parties. Unless we do so, our children, sitting in racially segregated classrooms, would be more than justified in thinking us hypocrites, pretending to celebrate a school integration decision that our nation has spent a half-century evading. ∎

Many white people are tired of hearing about 'black complaints.' They know ghettos exist. They know urban schools are often quite bad. A majority of whites are suburbanites who have escaped these problems.

resources for the most challenged schools to meet these demands. In fact, the Bush administration reneged on its promise to seek an additional $5.8 billion in funding for the poorest schools to meet the act's tough performance requirements. Even assuming that all promised extra funding were forthcoming, overcoming the oppositional culture that tends to permeate high-poverty environments cannot be done with mere dollars. Rhetoric and mandates are easy. Transforming urban education in school districts saddled with concentrated poverty and fewer resources is not.

If the answer to the problem of concentrated poverty in schools is breaking up those concentrations and sending more inner-city kids to suburban schools or attracting more middle-class kids to public schools through magnet and charter school programs, it is not clear that the great suburban majority—70 percent of voters now live in suburbs—will support this. Many white

people are tired of hearing about "black complaints." They know ghettos exist. They know urban schools are often quite bad. A majority of whites are suburbanites who have escaped these problems.

One way to build support for more innovative responses to race and class separation in schooling is to educate the vast majority about the costs they directly bear under this system. Historically we have accepted inequality in our nation when it appeared that it was racial minorities, particularly black people, that were receiving unequal treatment. But middle-income whites who cannot afford private school tuition also suffer in this system. In a public school system that is essentially premised upon the notion that some children will fall behind, middle-class parents must be ever vigilant to make sure that their kids get in the right classes with the best teachers.

In a socioeconomically integrated system fundamentally committed to bring every child of whatever background along, parents would not have to fight so hard to ensure their child is not one of the ones who fall through the cracks. There would be less anxiety for everyone. White, middle-class anxiety will only increase as public school systems become more and more populated with disadvantaged minority kids. Those who cannot escape to private school or "safe" havens of white affluence will pay a price, just as the minority kids do, in schools systems that have failed to figure out how to educate all kids.

American life is hard. Both parents, if there are two of them, feel compelled to work. Raising children well seems a challenge.

Affording the safest path to a middle-class existence for one's child seems to require choosing separation either in the form of private school or a more homogeneous neighborhood that offers "good" schools. There are often quality alternatives within even challenged public school systems, but it might require a white parent to be willing to place her child in a school where the child is outnumbered by students from other racial and ethnic backgrounds. White colleagues of mine who have pursued this road less traveled have found quality alternatives that enable both their children and, dare I say it, other people's children, to thrive.

In the din of debate about what can work to ensure a quality educational experience for all children, a small movement for economic integration has been emerging. About two dozen school districts, from Cambridge, Mass., to St. Lucie County, Fla., have adopted "controlled choice" plans that attempt to ensure that no school is overwhelmed by poverty. I think this is the right focus of the debate, although I am aware that these strategies swim against a tide of parental skeptics who are not much interested in integration.

Where will the political will to solve the "hard" problems surrounding public education come from? It will come, I hope, from an ethos of togetherness that we need to cultivate, lest the public, common good be completely sacrificed, and those disadvantaged at birth left to falter in inadequate public schools. Herein lies the rub. Unless more middle-class students, including white students, enter into the multicultural fray, we are doomed to a status quo of increasing segregation, and inequality. ■

Social Class Leaves Its Imprint

BY RICHARD ROTHSTEIN

Richard Rothstein is the author of *Class and Schools*, published jointly this spring by Teachers College, Columbia University, and the Economic Policy Institute (epinet.org).

T he 50th anniversary of the U.S. Supreme Court's desegregation decision evokes a sense of national failure. Few whites and blacks mingle in schools, and a big achievement gap remains. Blacks do worse than whites, even when family incomes are similar. Most Americans find this puzzling and assume that schools must not try very hard to teach black youngsters.

But the problem has been poorly defined, making solutions unlikely. The achievement gap has two parts. First, black children perform less well than whites, on average, because blacks are more likely to be lower-class—poor and with other social and economic disadvantages. Second, black children perform worse than whites even from the same social class.

Because class is so hard to define, we can't know precisely how important each of these might be. But as we statistically control for more social and economic characteristics, not income alone, the remaining race achievement gap gets smaller. Most of it is a social-class gap, unlikely to be closed unless differences in the conditions of lower- and middle-class children can be narrowed.

For example, parents of different social classes often have different child-rearing styles. It makes sense when you think about it: If upper-middle-class parents have jobs where they are expected to collaborate with fellow employees or create new solutions to problems, they are more likely to talk to their children in open-ended ways that differ from how parents address children if their own jobs simply require following orders. Children raised by middle-class parents will, on average, have more inquisitive attitudes toward academic material than children raised by working-class parents. No matter how competent a schoolteacher, lower-class children's achievement will, on average, almost inevitably be less. Because the achievement gap already exists by age 3, it is unlikely to be narrowed without expensive infant and toddler centers where lower-class children can be exposed to the language of highly educated adults.

Health differences also affect learning. Lower-class children have twice the rate of poor vision of middle-class children, partly from prenatal conditions, partly from how their eyes are trained as infants and toddlers, with more television watching and fewer manipulative toys. They have poorer oral hygiene, more lead poisoning, more asthma, poorer nutrition, and less-adequate pediatric care. Each of these well-documented social-class characteristics may have a small effect for any child, but each palpably influences academic achievement; combined, their influence grows.

Consider that poor children have more dental cavities than middle-class children (three times as many, in fact). If you gave a test to two otherwise identical groups, one of which had more children with toothaches, wouldn't you expect the healthier group to have higher average scores?

Or consider asthma. Studies of black children in New York City and Chicago find that one-fourth suffer from asthma, a rate six times that for all children. The disease is provoked in part from breathing fumes from low-grade home heating oil and from diesel trucks and buses.

Asthma keeps children up at night and, if they make it to school, they are likely to be drowsy and inattentive. Middle-class children typically get asthma treatment; low-income children get it less often. Low-income children with asthma are about 80 percent more likely than middle-class children with asthma to miss more than seven days of school a year from the disease. No matter how good a school, if it has more asthmatic children it will have lower scores than

More nuanced understanding of black and white children's social-class characteristics not only helps explain why an achievement gap persists, but also points to solutions that are rarely contemplated in education debates today.

others, other things being equal.

Growing housing unaffordability for low-income families also affects learning. Children whose families can't find stable housing change schools frequently. Teachers, no matter how well trained, can't be as effective with children who move in and out of their classrooms. Black children are more than twice as likely as whites to have attended at least three different schools by the 3rd grade. If black children's mobility were reduced to the rate of whites, part of the black-white gap would disappear from this change alone.

Differences in economic security also influence student achievement, but we overlook many of these differences when we focus only on annual income to indicate disadvantage. Black families with low income in any year are likely to have been poor for longer than white families with low income in that year. A family's poverty when children are young influences their achievement on into high school. With black families more likely to be permanently poor, the achievement of low-income black adolescents, on average, will be lower than that of low-income white adolescents. They will seem economically similar, but not be so.

White families typically own more assets that support children's achievement than black families with similar income. (Blacks and whites save at the same rate, but whites have accumulated capital for longer.) Black median family income is now about 64 percent of whites', but blacks' median family assets are only 12 percent of whites'. This makes college less affordable for black than white children, even from families with similar incomes. It stands to reason that children who know their parents can send them to college will have higher aspirations. This may not be a big factor, but the achievement gap is composed of many tiny differences like this.

There are also cultural characteristics that contribute a bit to the black-white gap. A black culture of underachievement is widely discussed and little understood. But one aspect is easy to understand. Because of ongoing labor-market discrimination, education pays off less for blacks than for whites, especially for males who are high school but not college graduates. In a recent study, trained black and white young men delivered applications for advertised jobs requiring only a high school education. Their résumés were similar, except half mentioned a drug conviction. Whites with criminal records got called for interviews more often than blacks who were clean.

Black high school students know the challenges they face in the labor market, often saying they have to be twice as good as whites to get the same opportunities. Of course, we want black students to respond to this insight by studying twice as hard, but not all will do so. If even some reduce effort because they believe it won't pay off, the average achievement of blacks and whites will differ, even when other traits are the same.

More nuanced understanding of black and white children's social-class characteristics not only helps explain why an achievement gap persists, but points to solutions that are rarely contemplated in education debates today. It's not that school improvement isn't needed. It's that without social and economic reform as well, school improvement will be stymied.

Recall, for example, that many poor children can't read because they can't see. Putting optometric clinics in schools might generate bigger academic gains than many educational reforms we spend so much energy disputing. Dental clinics might do the same. So might enforcing regulations against low-grade heating oil in low-income communities. So might a host of other social and economic programs, large and small, that narrow the achievement gap by getting children to school more ready to learn.

If we try to narrow the gap with school reform alone, we're bound to be as disappointed 50 years from now as we are today. ■